PC

THE
GREAT WAR
ILLUSTRATED
1918

THE GREAT WAR ILLUSTRATED
1918

A selection of 1,000 images illustrating the Zeebrugge and Ostend raids; the German Spring Offensives; Salonika, Mesopotamia and Palestine; the Italian front; battles of the Aisne and Marne; the Americans at Cantigny, Château-Thierry, St Mihiel, Meuse-Argonne; the Battle of Amiens, the Hindenburg Line; Advance to Victory

William Langford & Jack Holroyd

Pen & Sword
MILITARY

Dedicated to the One True Sovereign
who was disregarded by the nations when, in 1914, men elected to fight
among themselves on behalf of their own sovereignties

First published in Great Britain in 2018 by
PEN & SWORD MILITARY

Pen & Sword Books Ltd.
47 Church Street, Barnsley,
South Yorkshire.
S70 2AS

ISBN 978 1 47388 165 5

The right of William Langford & Jack Holroyd to be identified as Authors of this Work
has been asserted by them in accordance with the
Copyright, Designs and Patents Act 1988.

A CIP catalogue record for this book is available
from the British Library

Designed by Factionpress
Printed and bound in India by Replika Press Pvt. Ltd.

Pen & Sword Books Ltd incorporates the imprints of
Pen & Sword Aviation, Pen & Sword Maritime,
Pen & Sword Military, Pen & Sword Select, Pen & Sword Military Classics,
Leo Cooper, Wharncliffe Local History

For a complete list of Pen & Sword titles please contact:
PEN & SWORD BOOKS LIMITED
47 Church Street, Barnsley, South Yorkshire, S70 2AS, England.
E-mail: enquiries@pen-and-sword.co.uk
Website: www.pen-and-sword.co.uk

Contents

Foreword

by Nigel Cave

The Great War Illustrated 1918

1918 turned out to be the last year of the war. Such an outcome was far from obvious when the year began. Admittedly the Central Powers were facing major problems on their southern flank, with the campaign in Palestine going badly, ending with the fall of Jerusalem in December. On the other hand, the fighting against Russia had ceased and the Germans (and Austrians) could look forward to reaping the peace dividend once a treaty was signed – which it was at Brest-Litovsk in March. This provided for very harsh treatment of the new Bolshevik regime (something that might be borne in mind when considering the treatment of Germany and her allies when they had lost the war). Whilst it is far from true to say that the Germans could transfer all their troops in the East to the West, it was certainly possible to remove the most capable and efficient formations. The German high command now had the manpower to prepare for a major, war winning offensive; and it had to be done quickly: her allies, Austria-Hungary, Bulgaria and Turkey, were showing signs of buckling under the strain.

1917 had been a year of major efforts by the allies in the west: at Arras, on the Chemin des Dames and at Third Ypres, popularly known as Passchendaele. The result of these had been, to put it mildly, disappointing. In the east, on the Russian Front, Kerensky's Provisional Government's (Kornilov) offensive of July had ended in disaster. The only thing preventing the Germans and Austrians advancing further than the 150 miles achieved was the challenge to their logistics. The weak government succumbed to the general chaos and the single-mindedness of Lenin and Trotsky; by mid December an armistice had been declared. In Italy a massive attack by the Central Powers at Caporetto (mid October to mid November 1917) had caused a rout of the Italians, which was only halted by a major effort and the promised deployment of masses of French and British troops to bolster their ally. Even the one, initial, bright moment for the allies, the attack at Cambrai, with its massed use of tanks, had been quickly extinguished by the well-organised German counter offensive which, whilst not fulfilling the hopes that had been put on it, had more or less restored the line where it was before the attack commenced.

Despite these setbacks for the Entente Powers, however, there were several important developments that caused the German government severe concern. Above all, there was the American declaration of war in April 1917. On paper, from a military point of view, this was not too much of an issue, at least at first: the American army was relatively small (smaller than Portugal's for example); it was completely inexperienced as regards modern war as being fought on the Western Front; the nation was unprepared (the American President, Wilson, had refused to allow the US General Staff even to plan for a US intervention); and it was very poorly equipped. However, this state of affairs would not continue for long and the Germans had to act before the sheer wealth and manpower resources that the USA provided the allied cause became a determining factor in the outcome of the war. A second problem was that the Royal Navy had, by the end of the year, managed to control the submarine threat by the employment of the convoy system; whilst losses of merchant shipping continued, it would seem that the tide had turned against this German strategic ploy. It had also become clear, at least to the directing staffs that the idea of holding strongly fortified series of lines had had its day. Third Ypres had proved that profligate use of concrete and steel in the construction of bunkers gave a false sense of security; whilst Cambrai, albeit that it was at best a draw, proved that even the formidable Hindenburg Line and its associated defences were vulnerable to the mass use of artillery and to tanks. Finally, Germany faced a resources crisis: one of these, manpower, was shared with the allies – but they had the advantage that the United States, given time, would provide a massive influx of men to the fighting on the Western Front. The second was that the blockade of the Central Powers meant that not only food was in short supply but also the raw materials required to feed the demands of the war machine.

The pendulum was swinging from favouring the defence to the offence: any new strategic planning would now move from the doctrine of a war of attrition back to the original one followed by both sides at the outbreak of the war, one of annihilation. Finally, 1918 found both sides facing a manpower crisis.

The Germans launched their attack in late March 1918; it aimed at splitting the British and French armies, possibly pushing the British back to the Channel Ports and, whilst not necessarily resulting in an outright military victory, might force the allies to a peace that was acceptable to the Germans. The attack was no great surprise. Apart from a restructuring of the BEF in early 1918 that became necessary because of the shortage of available manpower – whether because of the shortage of men from home or because Lloyd George withheld them, the British too had largely abandoned the idea of defence based on firmly held trenches. Indeed, defence was a new experience for the British, after years of being almost exclusively on the offensive. The solution was a wide battle zone, held by fortified strong points. It was the right option (especially as Haig had been forced to take on more of the line from the French); and, in the end, the line held. Not, however, before the situation had threatened to become extremely serious. Foch had been made the allied supremo, a rather vague responsibility, whose powers were never clearly delineated: however, with good will, the system worked very well.

Despite receiving a series of hard hits, by July it was clear to all that the Germans had failed to deliver anything like a knock out blow. Showing remarkable resilience, the BEF, in particular, and the French were able to launch a series of coordinated offensives that left the Germans reeling. By July there were sufficient American troops to play an important part in halting the German advance; and in the autumn over a million US troops took part in the Advance to Victory, most notably at the Battle of the Meuse-Argonne in late September, October and November (though at great cost). With revolution in the air at home, the economy in a shambles, her allies all defeated and the army in disarray, the new German republican government had no choice but to seek an armistice.

Although the war might be over, however, the world endured massive loss of life in 1918-19 as a result of the Spanish 'flu pandemic: at the least, estimated deaths attributed to it were twice as many, at the worst five times as many, as those who died as a result of the Great War. The legacy of the war was political and social instability in Europe and ruined economies. A thinking person would have had little to rejoice about, except for the ending of the war, on 11 November 1918.

Nigel Cave

Acknowledgements

With the completion of this, the fifth volume, it is appropriate that mention is made of those who have supported the task of publication. Reproduction quality of the 5,500 plus researched and corrected images is down to the Publisher, Charles Hewitt, who not only recognized the value to posterity of recording the Great War in picture-strip fashion and commissioning the work in the first place, but made sure that the finished result reflected the value to the Company Book List by selecting a quality printing company.

Because of the complexity of the subject of the First World War, the editor needed to be a scholar of experience, knowing the history of the period at an unusually high and competent level: Nigel Cave is the editor of the World War One books in the Battleground Europe series and worked with this author for thirty years on books for Pen & Sword. It was Nigel who, along with Jon Cooksey and this author, originated the Battleground series of visitor guide books. Nigel is a published author with upwards of twenty titles in print and has unselfishly assisted in the works of other writers. He is a founder member of the Durand Group (a fraternal association researching subterranean military mining systems, tunnels, subways, dugouts and bunkers; and other underground structures). Nigel also has worked for some years with Veterans Affairs Canada. When Matt Jones, the Production Manager at Pen & Sword, secured the services of Nigel Cave as editor for the GREAT WAR ILLUSTRATED series, this author was relieved. He was further delighted that Nigel would write a foreword, beginning with the 1916 volume. It is so easy to make a mistake and convey erroneous information (disputed casualty figures for example); thankfully Nigel has straightened me out on a number of wobbly occasions. He has contributed to this series by loaning books from his extensive library and suggested publications as sources for reference.

The colouring of original black and white photographs has added to the sparse number of coloured images available from the beginning of the twentieth century. This is down to the skill developed by Jon Wilkinson. Book designers and media programme producers have already used his work to 'lift' and vary their television productions. Jon's section adds variety to the overall presentation of the thousands of images on offer in these five volumes.

Technology leaves me reeling and support is down to the excellent staff at Pen & Sword: David Hemmingway and Dominic Allen who, over the years, have shown remarkable self-control and kindness when being pestered with the same old questions; and Alan and Mark Crossland, who can get me out of trouble by operating my terminal at home from three miles away – amazing!

Matt Jones, already mentioned, seems to possess a staggering ability to control and drive on all the elements in book production from cantankerous writers, to printing companies across the world, to copy editors and book commissioning editors; most publications pass across his chaotic desk top. His office staff are very supportive.

Fellow commissioning editor, Brigadier Henry Wilson, has always been a good-natured support over the years and during the production of this work.

Thanks also to support from across the water, from David Ginsburg and Jimmy Kilbourne (116th Infantry Regiment Foundation), who sought out and supplied a vital image.

Roni Wilkinson
January 2018

Chapter One: **Zeebrugge and Ostend Raids – Naval War**

18GW001 German marine infantry manning positions on the Belgian coast. Raids by the allies were expected.

18GW002 Old cruisers were to be used as block ships in the raid on the German bases; here they are being converted at Chatham Docks.

1918
10

The port of Zeebrugge fell into German hands in the autumn of 1914, and, with the neighbouring port of Ostend, soon became a thorn in the side of the British, French and Belgians by reason of its increasing use as a base for destroyers and submarines. Canals connected the inland port of Bruges with Zeebrugge and Ostend along which *Unterseeboot*, u-boats, destroyers and torpedo boats sailed from their pens at Bruges along the canal to the open sea at Zeebrugge to prey on the busy shipping lanes. Zeebrugge was especially useful, protected as it was from the rough sea by a crescent-shaped mole thirty feet high enclosing the harbour.

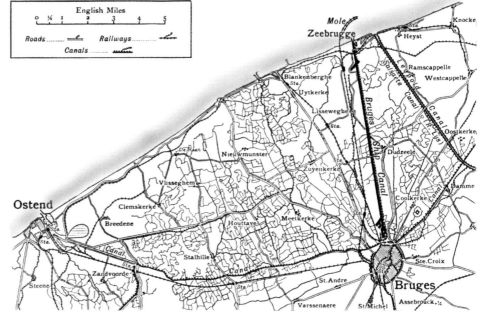

18GW012, 18GW007, 18GW006. The busy Belgian port of Zeebrugge, which served as a base for German submarines, minelayers and destroyers operating in the North Sea and English Channel. Concrete submarine pens along the canal at Bruges ensured protection against attack from the air.

18GW011 A German submarine returning to the *Kapersnest*, 'Pirates' Lair', at Zeebrugge. The camera has caught the strain on the faces of this crew. The original German caption could be translated as 'the hideous crew of a U-boat'.

18GW005 German V class torpedo boats steaming up at Zeebrugge.

18GW004 Maintenance of anti-submarine nets at Zeebrugges.

18GW008 German marines of one of the Flanders divisions riding through Zeebrugge. More effecient and cheaper than cavalry, these soldiers manage to keep in impeccable formation.

18GW010 Crew inspection on the aft port side deck of a torpedo boat destroyer at Zeebrugge. This type carried a crew of ninety-eight to one hundred officers and men.

18GW013, 18GW014 Submarine U-B *10* leaving the pens at Bruges and passing through the canal to Zeebrugge. It carried two torpedos only and was mainly used in coastal waters.

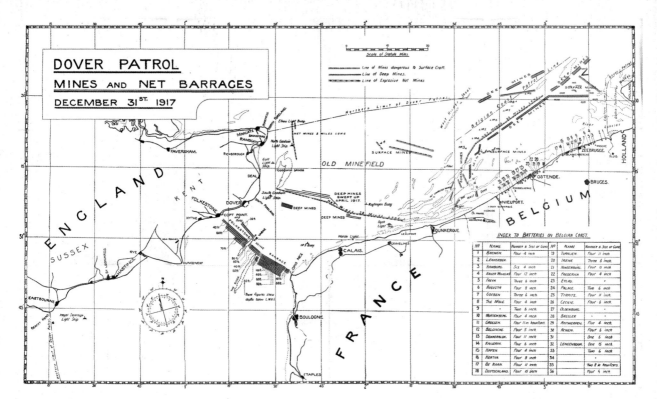

The Dover Patrol was a unit of the Royal Navy based at Dover and Dunkirk during the First World War. Its main task was to prevent German shipping – mainly submarines – from entering the English Channel en route to the Atlantic Ocean, thereby forcing German naval vessels to travel the longer route around Scotland, where the Royal Navy Northern Patrol operated to hinder their passage. It performed several duties in the Southern North Sea and the Dover Straits, which included: anti-submarine patrols; escorting merchantmen, hospital and troop ships; laying sea-mines and constructing mine barrages; and sweeping up German mines. Among its many duties it was responsible for bombarding German military positions on the Belgian coast, which incuded the outlets for Germany's submarines and destroyers at the ports of Ostend and Zeebrugge based at Bruges.

18GW017 Admiral Sir Reginald Hugh Spencer Bacon. He became Commander-in-Chief, Dover and commander of the Dover Patrol from 1915 until his replacement by Vice Admiral Sir Roger Keyes in January 1918.

18GW019 Royal Navy monitors bombarding Ostend from behind a smoke screen laid down by motor launches. Despite the cover, a cloud of cordite smoke from one of the ships' guns can be seen above, revealing the position of the monitors to the Geman batteries.

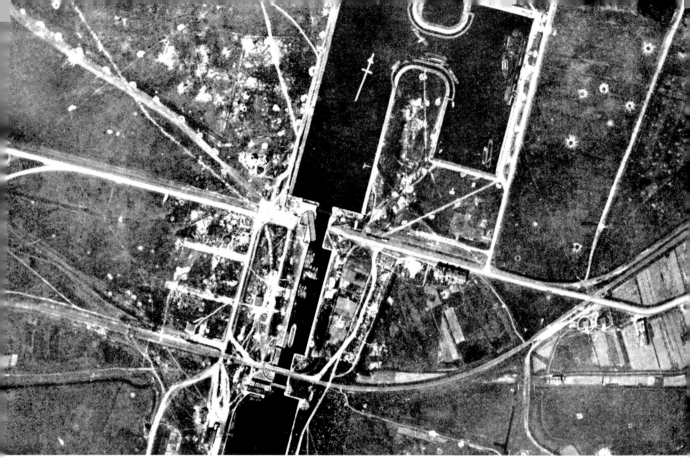

18GW020 The all-important large canal lock at Zeebrugge, with German submarines moored along the dockside; the aerial photograph was taken in May 1917 and shows shell and bomb cratering. Following an intensive bombardment on 16 May 1917 the lock itself was no longer used as a base.

18GW022 HMS *Sir John Moore*, a monitor of the Lord Clive class. Main armament consisted of two 12 inch guns from disarmed battleships; two 12 pdrs; one 3 pdr anti-aircraft gun; four 4 inch guns added in 1918. Deck armour was six inches. Based at Dover for most of the war, she was used to bombard the German held ports of Zeebrugge and Ostend.

18GW021 The results of a bombardment carried out on Ostend, 22 September, 1917, showing the damaged floating dock which had been sunk (marked with a double xx). Ostend and Zeebrugge had to be neutralized denying German easy access to the English Channel.

On the night of 22-23 April, 1918, a British naval raiding party under Vice Admiral Sir Roger Keyes, aided by French destroyers, undertook to wreck the stone mole at Zeebrugge and to block the entrances to the canals both at Zeebrugge and at Ostend by sinking the hulks of old ships in the channels. The episode proved to be one of the most daring naval operations of the war.

The object was to put out of action the German guns on the mole, along with torpedo boats and submarine depots and a large seaplane base. Block ships would be sunk in the channels leading to the main base at Brugge.

Six obsolete British cruisers took part in the attack. They were the *Brilliant, Iphigenia, Sirius, Intrepid, Thetis*, and *Vindictive*. The first five of these were filled with concrete and were to be sunk in the entrances of the two ports. The *Vindictive*, working with two Mersey ferryboats *Daffodil* and *Iris*, carried storming and demolition parties to the Zeebrugge mole.

The attacking forces were composed of bluejackets and Royal Marines picked from the Grand Fleet and from naval and marine depots. The fighting at Zeebrugge lasted for one hour and British losses amounted to 588 men, officially reported as follows: Officers killed, 16; died of wounds, 3; missing, 2; wounded, 29. Men killed, 144; died of wounds, 25; missing, 14; wounded, 355.

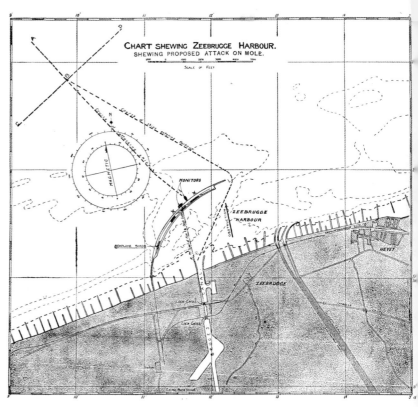

CHART SHEWING ZEEBRUGGE HARBOUR.
SHEWING PROPOSED ATTACK ON MOLE.

18GW024 A German battery of Pom-Pom automatic firing cannons at Zeebrugge; each weapon could fire 300 rounds per minute (rpm) for a distance of 4,500 yards.

18GW023 Vice Admiral Roger John Brownlow Keyes, Commander-in-Chief, Dover and commander of the Dover Patrol in January 1918. His predecessor, Admiral Bacon, had succeeded in sinking only two German submarines in the English Channel in two years, was out of an estimated 88,000 crossings by enemy ships. After Keyes took control, he introduced new tactics and the Dover Patrol sank five submarines in the first month.

18GW025 Target for the attack on Zeebrugge – 'The Mole'. This construction had no equal in Great Britain or the United States, it was one and a half miles long and was divided into four sections: the first, closest to shore, was a 300 yards long stone pier with double track railway lines; second was a connecting steel framed viaduct, which allowed the tidal current to pass in and out of the harbour; third was the mile-long, eighty yards wide main section made of concrete blocks topped with granite; fourth was a narrow section, ending with a lighthouse.

18GW026 The Mole pre-war, with day trippers seen here strolling along the first section; note the height of the sea wall, twenty feet high and over twelve feet thick.

18GW026 A low-level photograph of the dock gate of the Bruges canal. Attempts by the Allies to destroy this during the war failed.

18GW078 German seaplane base on the Mole at Zeebrugge.

18GW032 Barbed wire defences on the beach protecting The Mole should the Allies attempt to make a landing.

18GW031 The German Chief of the General Staff, Paul von Hindenburg, on a visit to the submarine base in Flanders. On his left is Ludwig von Schröder, commander of the *Marinekorps Flandern*, and his staff.

18GW048 Ostend blockship HMS *Brilliant*. Launched June 1891; scuttled at Ostend 23 April 1918. Attempt failed in its purpose.

18GW047 Ostend blockship HMS *Sirius*. Launched October 1890; scuttled at Ostend 23 April 1918. German defences effective, attack failed.

18GW046 Zeebrugge blockship HMS *Thetis*. Launched December 1890; scuttled at Zeebrugge 23 April 1918. Failed to block the waterway.

18GW044 Zeebrugge blockship HMS *Iphigenia*. Launched November 1891; scuttled at Zeebrugge 23 April 1918. Limited success in preventing submarines using the Brugges canal.

18GW044 Zeebrugge blockship HMS *Intrepid*. Launched June 1891; scuttled at Zeebrugge 23 April 1918. Limited success in preventing submarines using the Brugges canal.

18GW049 Zeebrugge attack submarine *C3*. Under the command of Lieutenant Sandford, the *C3*, filled with explosives, was to ram the viaduct connecting The Mole to the mainland and detonate. The crew of two officers and four men would make their escape in a small boat

18GW039 The main assault ship chosen was the armoured cruiser HMS *Vindictive* (launched 1897; sunk as a blockship at Ostend on 10 May 1918). Specially fitted out with supporting armament for the raid, this included: one 11 inch howitzer (mounted on the quarter deck); two 7.5 inch howitzers; two flamethrowers; two pom-pom cannons; sixteen Lewis guns; sixteen Stokes mortars. She retained her usual armament of four 6 inch guns and three pom poms.

The total number of personnel required for various aspects of the raid, including the block ships, amounted to 86 officers and 1,698 men *Vindictive* was only able to carry the First Wave of the assaulting force. The two shallow draught Mersey ferries carried the rest.

18GW034 The Mersey ferryboats *Iris* (right) and *Daffodil*, in the centre.

18GW036 Deck of the *Vindictive*, showing specially constructed gangplanks that could be lowered to connect with the Mole to discharge the raiding party.

18GW042 Royal Marines demonstrating their fighting garb. Much to the disappointment of many, they were issued with khaki for the raid.

18GW052 Men belonging to the crew of the battleship HMS *King George V* responding to the call for volunteers for a hazardous assignment. The response was such that not all who volunteered could be accepted. The Zeebrugge objective was not known at the time.

18GW055 The landing brows, or gangways, fitted on the assault ship *Vindictive* shortly before her departure for Zeebrugge.

18GW053 Captain Henry C. Halahan was in command of the naval storming party, comprising six officers and 150 men divided into three groups of fifty. Two groups sailed on the *Vindictive* and one on the *Iris*.

18GW056 The *Daffodil*, carrying her seamen demolition party and their covering party of twenty-two men from 4th Battalion Royal Marine Light Infantry

18GW054 Five Platoon, 4th Battalion Royal Marine Light Infantry, with Lieutenant Cooke.

18GW059 Smoke screen gear being demonstrated on the stern of the *Daffodil*.

18GW057 Officers of 4th Battalion Royal Marine Light Infantry. Out of the twenty-eight officers in this photograph taken before the raid, sixteen became casualties. The Officer Commanding, Lieutenant Colonel Elliot, is seated on the front row, centre; the Adjutant, Captain Charter, is seated to his left.

The Mersey ferries the *Daffodil* and the *Iris* were requisitioned in 1918 for the Zeebrugge raid. In preparation for the raid, all furniture and fittings were stripped and armour fitted to the superstructure of the *Iris* and *Daffodil*. The ferries were chosen because of their shallow draught and double hulls. They were towed into action by HMS *Vindictive*. The *Daffodil* was hit in the engine room by two shells, but was able to maintain her position, holding *Vindictive* against the wall of the Zeebrugge Mole where the raiding parties were disembarking. The *Iris* is seen here seen rigged for war, with armour plate sheets protecting the main deck.

18GW030 Barbed wire entanglements defending German positions on the Mole.

An artist's impression of Royal Marines storming up the specially constructed gang planks bridging between the deck of the *Vindictive* and the Mole wall.

After the battle British dead on the Mole parapet. The body in the foreground is thought to be that of Lieutenant Hawkings.

DEAN, Percy Thompson Lieutenant, Royal Naval Volunteer Reserve

For most conspicuous gallantry. Lieutenant Dean handled his boat [*ML 282*] in a most magnificent and heroic manner when embarking the officers and men from the block ships at Zeebrugge. He followed the block ships in and closed *Intrepid* and *Iphigenia* under a constant and deadly fire from machine and heavy guns at point blank range, embarking over 100 officers and men. This completed, he was proceeding out of the canal when he heard that an officer was in the water. He returned, rescued him, and then proceeded calmly as if engaged in a practice manoeuvre. Three men were shot down at his side whilst he conned his ship. On clearing the entrance to the canal, the steering gear broke down. He manoeuvred his boat by the engines, and avoided complete destruction by steering so close in under the Mole that the guns in the batteries could not depress sufficiently to fire on the boat. The whole of this operation was carried out under constant machine-gun fire at a few yards' range. It was solely due to this officer's courage and daring that *ML 282* succeeded in saving so many valuable lives. *The London Gazette* 23 July 1918. **Victoria Cross.**

CARPENTER, Alfred Francis Blakeney Commander, Royal Navy

For most conspicuous gallantry. This officer was in command of *Vindictive*. He set a magnificent example to all those under his command by his calm composure when navigating mined waters, bringing his ship alongside the Mole in darkness. When *Vindictive* was within a few yards of the Mole, the enemy started and maintained a heavy fire from batteries, machine guns and rifles onto the bridge. He showed most conspicuous bravery, and did much to encourage similar behaviour on the part of the crew, supervising the landing from *Vindictive* on to the Mole, and walking round the decks directing operations and encouraging the men in the most dangerous and exposed positions. By his encouragement to those under him, his power of command and personal bearing, he undoubtedly contributed greatly to the success of the operation. *The London Gazette* 19 July 1918. **Victoria Cross.**

BRADFORD, George Nicholson Lieutenant Commander, Royal Navy

For most conspicuous gallantry at Zeebrugge on the night of the 22nd-23rd April, 1918. This officer was in command of the Naval Storming Parties embarked in *Iris II*. When *Iris II* proceeded alongside the Mole great difficulty was experienced in placing the parapet anchors owing to the motion of the ship. An attempt was made to land by the scaling ladders before the ship was secured. Lieutenant Claude E. K. Hawkings (late *Erin*) managed to get one ladder in position and actually reached the parapet, the ladder being crushed to pieces just as he stepped off it. This very gallant young officer was last seen defending himself with his revolver. He was killed on the parapet. Though securing the ship was not part of his duties, Lieutenant Commander Bradford climbed up the derrick, which carried a large parapet anchor and was rigged out over the port side; during this climb the ship was surging up and down and the derrick crashing on the Mole. Waiting his opportunity he jumped with the parapet anchor on to the Mole and placed it in position. Immediately after hooking on the parapet anchor Lieutenant Commander Bradford was riddled with bullets from machine guns and fell into the sea between the Mole and the ship. Attempts to recover his body failed. Lieutenant Commander Bradford's action was one of absolute self-sacrifice; without a moment's hesitation he went to certain death, recognising that in such action lay the only possible chance of securing *Iris II* and enabling her storming parties to land. *The London Gazette* 14 March 1919. **Victoria Cross.**

BAMFORD, Edward DSO Captain, Royal Marine Light Infantry

For most conspicuous gallantry. This officer landed on the Mole from *Vindictive* with Numbers 5, 7, and 8 Platoons of the marine storming force, in the face of great difficulties. When on the Mole and under heavy fire he displayed the greatest initiative in the command of his company and by his total disregard of danger showed a magnificent example to his men. He first established a strongpoint on the right of the disembarkation and, when satisfied that that was safe, led an assault on the battery on the left with the utmost coolness and valour. *The London Gazette* 23 July 1918. **Victoria Cross.**

He died 30 September 1928, on board HMS *Cumberland* en route to Hong Kong.

FINCH, Norman Augustus Sergeant, Royal Marine Artillery

For most conspicuous gallantry. Sergeant Finch was second in command of the pompoms and Lewis guns in the foretop of *Vindictive* under Lieutenant Charles N.B. Rigby, RMA. At one period, the *Vindictive* was being hit every few seconds, chiefly in the upper works, from which splinters caused many casualties. It was difficult to locate the guns which were doing most damage but Lieutenant Rigby, Sergeant Finch and the marines in the foretop kept up a continuous fire with pompoms and Lewis guns, changing rapidly from one target to another and thus keeping the enemy's fire down to some considerable extent. Unfortunately, two heavy shells made direct hits on the foretop, which was completely exposed to enemy concentration of fire. All in the top were killed or disabled except Sergeant Finch, who was, however, severely wounded; nevertheless, he showed consummate bravery, remaining in this battered and exposed position. He once more got a Lewis gun into action, and kept up a continuous fire, harassing the enemy on the Mole, until the foretop received another direct hit, the remainder of the armament being then completely put out of action. Before the top was destroyed, Sergeant Finch had done invaluable work, and by his bravery undoubtedly saved many lives. *The London Gazette* 19 July 1918. **Victoria Cross**.

HARRISON, Arthur Leyland Lieutenant Commander, Royal Navy

Posthumous award of the Victoria Cross. For most conspicuous gallantry at Zeebrugge on the night of 22/23 April 1918. This officer was in command of the Naval Storming Parties embarked in *Vindictive*. Immediately before coming alongside the Mole Lieutenant Commander Harrison was struck on the head by a fragment of shell, which broke his jaw and knocked him senseless. Recovering consciousness, he proceeded onto the Mole and took over command of his party, who were attacking the seaward end of the Mole. The silencing of the guns on the Mole head was of the first importance and, though in a position fully exposed to the enemy's machine-gun fire, Lieutenant Commander Harrison gathered his men together and led the attack. He was killed at the head of his men, all of whom were either killed or wounded. Lieutenant Commander Harrison, though severely wounded, and undoubtedly in great pain, displayed indomitable resolution and courage of the highest order in pressing his attack, knowing as he did that any delay in silencing the guns might jeopardise the main object of the expedition i.e. the blocking of the Zeebrugge canal. *The London Gazette* 17 March 1919. **Victoria Cross.** He was an English Rugby International – the only one to win the VC.

McKENZIE, Albert Edward Able Seaman, Royal Navy

For most conspicuous gallantry. This rating belonged to B Company, a seaman storming party. On the night of the operation, he landed on the Mole with his machine gun in the face of great difficulties and did very good work, using his gun to the utmost advantage. He advanced down the Mole with Lieutenant Commander Harrison, who with most of his party was killed, and accounted for several of the enemy running from a shelter to a destroyer alongside the Mole. This very gallant seaman was severely wounded whilst working his gun in an exposed position. *The London Gazette* 19 July 1918. **Victoria Cross.**

SANDFORD, Richard Douglas Lieutenant, Royal Navy

For conspicuous gallantry. This officer was in command of submarine *C3*, and most skilfully placed that vessel in between the piles of the viaduct before lighting his fuse and abandoning her. He eagerly undertook this hazardous enterprise, although well aware (as were all his crew) that if the means of rescue failed and he or any of the crew were in the water at the moment of the explosion, they would be killed outright by the force of such an explosion. Yet Sandford disdained to use the gyro steering, which would have enabled him and his crew to abandon the submarine at a safe distance, and preferred to make sure, as far as humanly possible, of the accomplishment of his duty. *The London Gazette* 23 July 1918. **Victoria Cross.**

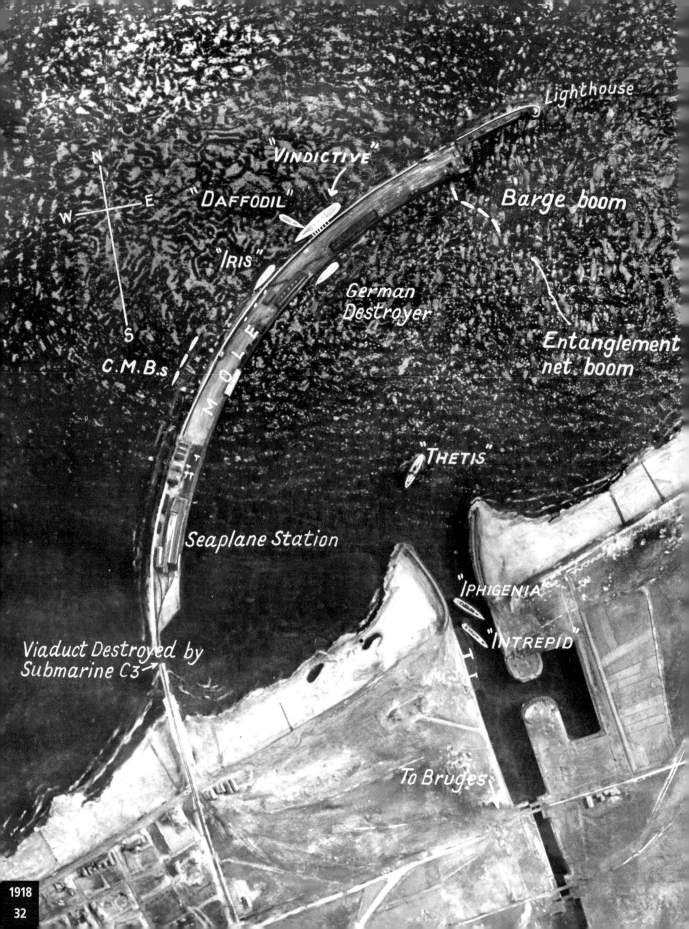

Lighthouse

"VINDICTIVE"

"DAFFODIL"

Barge boom

N
W — E
S

"IRIS"

German
Destroyer

Entanglement
net boom

M O L E

C.M.B.s

"THETIS"

Seaplane Station

"IPHIGENIA"

"INTREPID"

Viaduct Destroyed by
Submarine C3

To Bruges

18GW075 Lieutenant Richard Sandford placed submarine *C3*, which was packed with explosives, under the viaduct at Zeebrugge. The subsequent explosion destroyed the bridging section connecting the Mole with the mainland, thus denying an easy way for the Germans to reinforce their defenders fighting hand to hand with the raiders.

18GW073 Photograph of a model of the raid, with annotation overlayed.

18GW003 When the *Vindictive* withdrew for home, with her upper structure ripped by shrapel and riddled with bullet holes, she left behind on the Mole one officer and thirteen men. At first feigning death the men finally surrendered when a German officer called out to them: *Play the game lads and we will play the game with you. Lay down your arms and put your hands up and we will not harm you.* An official German photograph was taken of the other ranks made prisoners of the Kaiser.

18GW079, 18GW081. Smoke coming from the prow of the *Intrepid* at 11.00 hours, 23 April 1918, photograph taken by the Germans. The channel was completely blocked at low tide – note the sandbank; these could be crossed by submarines at high tide.

18GW080, 18GW076. Aerial view taken at high tide and looking north. Another view from the opposite direction looking southwards towards the lock gates and entrance to the Brugge canal at low tide.

18GW050, 18GW082. The substantial breach in the Mole viaduct, caused by 10,000 kilos of high explosive delivered with accuracy by the crew of C3 under the command of Lieutenant Richard Sandford.

Blockship *Intrepid* Blockship *Iphigenia* Blockship *Thetis*

Sandbank

Sandbank

18GW083 Ship movement was seriously impeded by the placing of the three blockships, although shallow-draught crsft could pass at high tide.

18GW085 Field Marshal von Hindenburg and Admiral von Schroeder paid a visit to Zeebrugge after the raid and commended the defenders.

18GW086 German gunners guarding the Mole. Taken by a German photographer after the raid.

18GW084 Crews of the *Schiffsartillerie* who manned the guns of the *Tirpitz* battery during the raid. They have each just received the Iron Cross for their action against the *Vindictive*.

18GW074 German officers decorated for bravery. The commander of the Mole battery, *Kapitanleutnant* Robert Shutte, is third from the right (two rings on forearm). Both sides decorated their heroes.

18GW077 HMS *Vindictive* sailed into Dover at 8 am on the morning of 23 April 1918 (St George's Day). Crowds cheered her arrival back from the raid; for some enthusiasm must have become subdued at the sight of the old cruiser's bullet and shrapnel riddled funnels and superstructure.

18GW040 HMS *Vindictive* on return from Zeebrugge, showing the bridge, fighting top and flame thrower position on the right. Beneath it is a Stokes mortar position.

18GW087 Some of the officers of *Vindictive* (left to right): Surgeon Payne, Surgeon Clegg, Commander E. Osborne, Captain A. F. Carpenter, Staff Surgeon G. McCutcheon and Assistant Paymaster E. G. Young.

18GW087 On the deck of the *Vindictive*, Captain A. F. Carpenter and Commander E. Osborne with some of her crew cheering for the photographer after the raid.

18GW094 Sorting through items used in the fighting: rifles; bayonets; respirators; and sheets of armour plating with rifle loop holes. The decks appear to be stained with blood.

18GW090, 18GW091, 18GW093. Massive clean-up operation on HMS *Vindictive*.

18GW095 The Stokes mortar position situated beneath the flamethrower hut on HMS *Vindictive*.

18GW035 Port side view of *Vindictive,* safely in Dover.

18GW088, 18GW048. The riddled funnels and superstructure on *Vindictive*. The signal for the raiders to withdraw from the Mole and make their escape was to have been the morse letter 'K' blown on the steam whistle; however, nothing worked because of the damage inflicted. *Daffodil* gave the signal to re-embark.

18GW060 The fighting top on *Vindictive* where Sergeant Finch earned his VC.

18GW097, 18GW098. Safely back in Dover, the *Iris* showing signs of the fierce fire from German machine guns and pompom canons that had swept her deck and bridge during the raid. The Wallasey ferry boats *Iris* and *Daffodil* returned to the River Mersey in May 1918 and were given a proud reception by the people.

SOUVENIR
OF THRILLING SERVICE BY THE
WALLASEY FERRY BOATS
H.M.S. IRIS II. and DAFFODIL IV.
IN THE

ZEEBRUGGE RAID

St. George's Day, 23rd April, 1918.

18GW096 Hasty repairs were made to the battered *Vindictive*: she was made ready in four days for a further attack on Ostend.

The map shows where the *Vindictive* ended up after the Germans succeeded in moving her so that she failed to block the channel. The raid on Ostend was a failure. The report at the time listed: *two officers and six men killed, five officers and twenty-five men wounded, two officers and nine men missing, believed killed*.

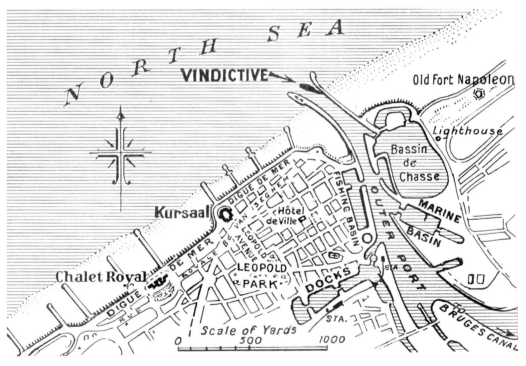

BOURKE, Rowland Richard Louis Lieutenant, Royal Naval Volunteer Reserve

Volunteered for rescue work in command of *ML 276*, and followed *Vindictive* into Ostend, engaging the enemy's machine guns on both piers with Lewis guns. After *ML 254* had backed out, Lieutenant Bourke laid his vessel alongside *Vindictive* to make further search. Finding no one, he withdrew, but hearing cries in the water he again entered the harbour and, after a prolonged search, eventually found Lieutenant Sir John Alleyane and two ratings all badly wounded in the water clinging to an upended skiff, and rescued them. During all the time the motor launch was under a heavy fire at close range, being hit in fifty-five places, once by a six-inch shell – two of her crew being killed and others wounded. The vessel was seriously damaged and speed greatly reduced. Lieutenant Bourke however managed to bring her out until he fell in with a Monitor, which took him in tow. This episode displayed daring and skill of a very high order, and Lieutenant Bourke's bravery and perseverance undoubtedly saved the lives of Lieutenant Alleyane and two of *Vindictive's* crew. *The London Gazette* 28 August 1918. **Victoria Cross.**

CRUTCHLEY, Victor Alexander Charles DSC Lieutenant, Royal Navy

This officer was in *Brilliant* in the unsuccessful attempt to block Ostend on the night of 22/23 April, and at once volunteered for a further effort. He acted as First Lieutenant of *Vindictive* and worked with untiring energy fitting out that ship for further service. On the night of 9/10 May, after his commanding officer had been killed and the second in command severely wounded, Lieutenant Crutchley took command of *Vindictive* and did his utmost by manoeuvring the engines to place that ship in an effective position. He displayed great bravery in both the *Vindictive* and *ML 254*, which rescued the crew after the charges had been blown and the former vessel sank between the piers of Ostend harbour, and did not leave the *Vindictive* until he had made a thorough search with an electric torch for survivors under a very heavy fire. Lieutenant Crutchley took command of *ML 254* when the commanding officer sank exhausted from his wounds, the second in command having been killed. The vessel was full of wounded and very seriously damaged by shell-fire, the fore part being flooded. With indomitable energy and by dint of baling with buckets and shifting weight aft, Lieutenant Crutchley and the unwounded kept her afloat, but the leaks could not be kept under, and she was in a sinking condition, with her forecastle nearly awash, when picked up by HMS *Warwick*. The bearing of this very gallant officer and fine seaman throughout these operations off the Belgian coast was altogether admirable and an inspiring example to all thrown in contact with him. *The London Gazette* 28 August 1918. **Victoria Cross.**

DRUMMOND, Geoffrey Heneage Lieutenant, Royal Naval Volunteer Reserve
Volunteered for rescue work in command of *ML 254*. Following *Vindictive* to Ostend, when off the piers a shell burst on board, killing Lieutenant Gordon Ross and Deckhand J. Thomas, wounding the coxswain, and severely wounding Lieutenant Drummond in three places. Notwithstanding his wounds, he remained on the bridge, navigated his vessel, already seriously damaged by shellfire, into Ostend harbour, placed her alongside *Vindictive* and took off two officers and thirty-eight men, some of whom were killed and many wounded while embarking. When informed there was no one alive left on board he backed his vessel clear of the piers before sinking exhausted from his wounds. When HMS *Warwick* fell in with *ML 254* off Ostend half an hour later the latter was in sinking condition. It was due to the indomitable courage of this very gallant officer that the majority of the crew of the *Vindictive* were rescued. *The London Gazette* 28 August 1918. **Victoria Cross.**

18GW037, 18GW101. The *Vindictive* against a pier at Ostend and clearly not blocking the channel. *The Times* newspaper announced the failure to the nation:

The Germans have been successful in shifting Vindictive's *position inside Ostend harbour; that she had been swung round so that she lay through her whole length close against the eastern pier, leaving a passage of about thirty feet comparatively free for vessels to go in or out; that is sufficient space for a destroyer of large size, though it would be difficult to get her through.*

18GW102 The deck of the *Vindictive* in the morning after the attempted blockade of Ostend. Germans survey the battered cruiser.

Information used in this chapter was based on the following title in the **Battleground Europe** series of guide books: ***Zeebrugge & Ostend Raids*** by Stephen McGreal

Chapter Two: **The German Spring Offensives – the *Kaiserschlacht***

18GW104 German *Sturmtruppen* preparing for the great Spring offensive that began on 21 March and ended on 17 July 1918.

18GW103 British and French troops falling back in good order before the German onslaught.

As 1917 ended the German high command found itself in a favourable position: The collapse of the Russian Army allowed the Germans to concentrate their best troops on the Western Front. Ludendorff began to prepare a massive attack to be launched in Spring 1918, before the American Expeditionary Force was sufficiently reinforced to present a real danger. The British Army, which the German strategists considered to be exhausted after four arguably fruitless offensives during 1917 at Arras, Messines, Passchendaele and Cambrai, would be the main target. Of the 110 German divisions stationed along the front line, fifty were allocated to the British sector.

18GW120 American divisions were arriving in europe in ever increasing numbers.

18GW115 *Generalfeldmarcshall* Paul von Hindenburg and *General der Infanterie* Erich von Ludendorff (pointing) on the occasion of Hindenburg's 70th birthday celebration, October 1917. They would have to deliver a significant defeat on the weakened British before the Americans tipped the scales against them.

Due largely to the transfer of troops from the east, in just five months German troop strengths in the west had increased by 30%. On the other hand, since the wasting battles of Passchendaele, British infantry strengths had decreased by 20%. Haig and his generals were content to await the arrival of fresh American troops before considering any further offensives in 1918.

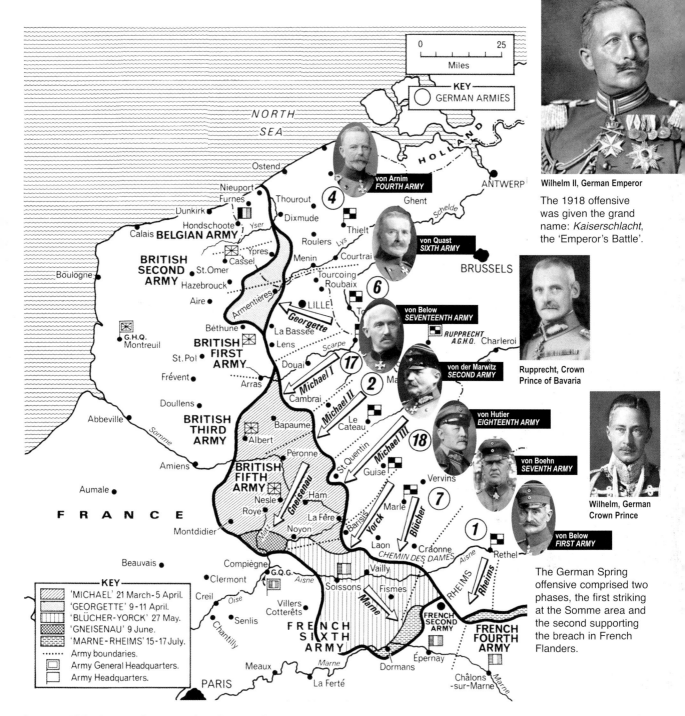

NORTH SEA

Ostend

Nieuport
Furnes
Thourout
Ghent
Dunkirk
Dixmude
HOLLAND
ANTWERP

Calais
Hondschoote
Thielt
Ypres
Roulers
Menin
Courtrai
BRUSSELS

BELGIAN ARMY

Boulogne
BRITISH SECOND ARMY
St.Omer
Cassel
Hazebrouck
Aire
Tourcoing
Roubaix

von Arnim
FOURTH ARMY

4

von Quast
SIXTH ARMY

6

Wilhelm II, German Emperor

The 1918 offensive was given the grand name: *Kaiserschlacht*, the 'Emperor's Battle'.

Armentieres
LILLE
Georgette
Béthune
La Bassée
G.H.Q. Montreuil
BRITISH FIRST ARMY
Lens
St.Pol
Douai
Frévent
Arras
Michael I
Cambrai

von Below
SEVENTEENTH ARMY

17

RUPPRECHT
A.G.H.Q.
Charleroi

Rupprecht, Crown Prince of Bavaria

Doullens
BRITISH THIRD ARMY
Bapaume
Albert
Peronne
Michael II
Le Cateau

2

von der Marwitz
SECOND ARMY

Amiens
Somme
Aumale
BRITISH FIFTH ARMY
Nesle
Roye
Ham
La Fère
Gneisenau
St.Quentin
Guise

von Hutier
EIGHTEENTH ARMY

18

Michael III

von Boehn
SEVENTH ARMY

Wilhelm, German Crown Prince

FRANCE
Montdidier
Noyon
Laon
Craonne
CHEMIN DES DAMES
Rethel
Yorck
Blücher
Marle
Vervins

7

1

von Below
FIRST ARMY

Beauvais
Compiègne
G.Q.G.
Aisne
Soissons
Vailly
Fismes
RHEIMS
Aisne
Rheims

The German Spring offensive comprised two phases, the first striking at the Somme area and the second supporting the breach in French Flanders.

Clermont
Creil
Villers Cotterêts
Senlis
Chantilly
FRENCH SIXTH ARMY
Marne
FRENCH SECOND ARMY
FRENCH FOURTH ARMY
Épernay

Meaux
Marne
Dormans
Châlons-sur-Marne
PARIS
La Ferté

KEY
- 'MICHAEL' 21 March-5 April.
- 'GEORGETTE' 9-11 April.
- 'BLÜCHER-YORCK' 27 May.
- 'GNEISENAU' 9 June.
- 'MARNE-RHEIMS' 15-17 July.
- Army boundaries.
- Army General Headquarters.
- Army Headquarters.

KEY
GERMAN ARMIES

0   25
Miles

Operation Michael was the first stage of the German offensive and it was expected that the British front at Arras would be penetrated and, after swinging north, supply lines would be severed. It was anticipated that the resulting envelopment of British forces would secure their surrender. The section of the front chosen for the offensive had recently been taken over by the British from their French allies. The line left by the French was discovered to be poorly constructed for defence and the British had to substantially improve its fortifications. These works had barely commenced when the Germans struck on the 21 March 1918.

Casualties were considerable for both sides: the British lost 236,000 men killed, wounded and taken prisoner between 21 March and 29 April 1918. Number of killed amounted to 20,000; taken prisoner 120,000. The French suffered fewer losses 92,000, although the proportion of deaths was high for the units fighting on Kemmel Hill. The Germans lost 348,000 men over the same period.

Operation Michael was launched 21 March 1918; although anticipated, the tactics surprised the British troops who bore the brunt of the assault. Using to great effect their numerical superiority – fifty-eight attacking divisions against sixteen divisions defending – the Germans broke through the British front within hours. Several divisions were severely mauled, among them the Irish 16th, the 36th and the 66th. Other British units made a fighting retreat through the growing chaos of congested roads. Amiens soon came under threat and forced the British to commit large numbers of reserves to fill the breach.

18GW123 German reinforcements advancing during the initial assault on the British positions.

18GW124 A soldier of a Württemburg shock unit.

18GW122 A battery of tractor drawn 21 cm *mörser* moving up to new postions during the opening phases of the German offensive.

18GW129 A 77 mm field gun being moved forward. Attack divisions were supplied with 14,500 horses for the offensive.

18GW131 A medium trench mortar triggered with a lanyard, the crew standing well back.

18GW130, 18GW132. A highly mobile light trench mortar issued in time for the *Kaiserschlact*. A battery in training before the attack.

18GW128, 18GW126.
German shock and
assault troops cutting
through the enemy wire
for the infantry to
advance.

18GW127 Shock troops
advancing in assault
groups.

18GW125 Artillery pieces
driving through channels
cut in the barbed wire
defences.

18GW133, 18GW134. Two frames of a firing sequence of an L/27 Krupp, which was a modified 77 mm field gun fitted with smaller trail and wheels. It had been developed as a counter against allied tanks.

18GW136, 18GW135. Light trench mortar for infantry support, the 7.58 cm *minenwerfer*. The number of mortars issued for the offensive was 3,532.

18GW139 Artillery battery in action during *Operation Michael.* The number of artillery pieces committed to the offensive amounted to 6,473 of all calibres.

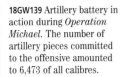

18GW137 German shock troops wearing white arm bands to help identify them from the enemy in the smoke and chaos of battle.

18GW140 German troops resting before deploying for the attack.

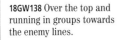

18GW138 Over the top and running in groups towards the enemy lines.

1918
58

18GW142, 18GW143. German shock troops advancing after breaking through barbed wire. These would likely be training photographs.

18GW147 *Feldmarschal* Paul von Hindenburg and General Ludendorff on the steps of a building close to the front. By this time both officers had become, effectively, the rulers of Germany, with the Kaiser acting as the nation's figurehead.

18GW149 Horses and rider wearing protection against poisonous gas. They are part of an ammunition column advancing near the city of Reims. Horses and mules proved unmanageable when attempts were made to shield their eyes.

18GW148 Part of a German artillery battery being towed into a firing postion, March-April 1918.

18GW145, 18GW146.
German troops in the
square in the Place de la
Republique, Armentières
prior to the launching of
the Lys offensive in April
1918.

18GW150 Narrow gauge
railway transporting
reinforcements to the
front line.

18GW151 Men of a
Stosskompanien (Shock
company) near
Sarrebourg.

18GW160 A German 21 cm howitzer being manoeuvred into position to be harnessed to a horse team.

18GW162 Men of a *Stosskompanien*, passing through a hastely errected street barricade in Bailleul.

18GW161 A German naval gun firing on Allied positions.

18GW166 German shock troops in the attack.

18GW163 Germans in open country don gas masks during an attack; note the soldier directing a war dog to the rear.

18GW164 A mortar team advancing across open country.

18GW165 German machine gunners in open fields near Ypres during the Lys offensive.

18GW168, 18GW176, 18GW173, 18GW174, 18GW175, 18GW176, British positions bombarded, overrun and captured by German *Sturmtruppen* during the opening stages of *Operation Michael*. The number of British Short Lee Enfield rifles scattered about in the bottom picture would seem to indicate a sudden surprise and capture of this position by the German storm troops.

18GW179 Uhlans mopping up during the advance and passing a taken British position.

18GW177 British prisoners.

18GW181 British removing horses and mules from a supplies depot set on fire to prevent stores falling into the hands of the advancing Germans.

18GW182 A captured British stores dump being riffled by German soldiers. Staple tinned foods were as luxuries to the German troops, who were suffering chronic food shortages. The German civilian population were strictly rationed and seriously malnuorished by 1918.

18GW180 Germans advancing through the outskirts of Bapaume during the March offensive. They had been driven from the town in the spring of 1917 and were back in possession one year later. They would be dislodged again in August during Haig's Advance to Victory.

18GW183 British troops of a Scottish regiment await the advancing Germans.

18GW186 A group of Gordon Highlanders in an old trench near Nesle prepared to take on the advancing *Sturmtruppen* during the March offensive.

18GW189, 18GW191 British and French troops side by side await the advancing Germans.

18GW192, 18GW193, 18GW194. Moving an 18 pounder into position to bring down fire on advancing Germans at the Lys canal.

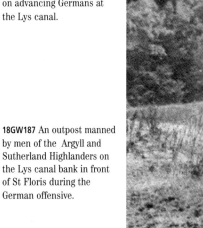

18GW187 An outpost manned by men of the Argyll and Sutherland Highlanders on the Lys canal bank in front of St Floris during the German offensive.

18GW158 One of the many photographs released to the press showing French and British soldiers together. With news of the Allies being driven back by the Germans and Paris once more in the firing line, propaganda images were needed to remind people that all would be well. Appropriate captions were supplied: *A photograph in the trenches where the French and British are side by side.* Issued in March 1918 during the German offensive.

18GW157 Canadians soldiers of the 87th Battalion CEF resting in a trench at Willerval near Vimy, 1 April 1918. During the German offensive at the end of March the 87th were part of the Canadian Corps in General Sir Henry Horne's First Army, which was holding the line between Lens and a point opposite Bailleul. The 87th were known as the 'Canadian Grenadier Guards'.

18GW159 French reinforcements were sent to support the hard-pressed British. French and British troops digging in together in the Somme region.

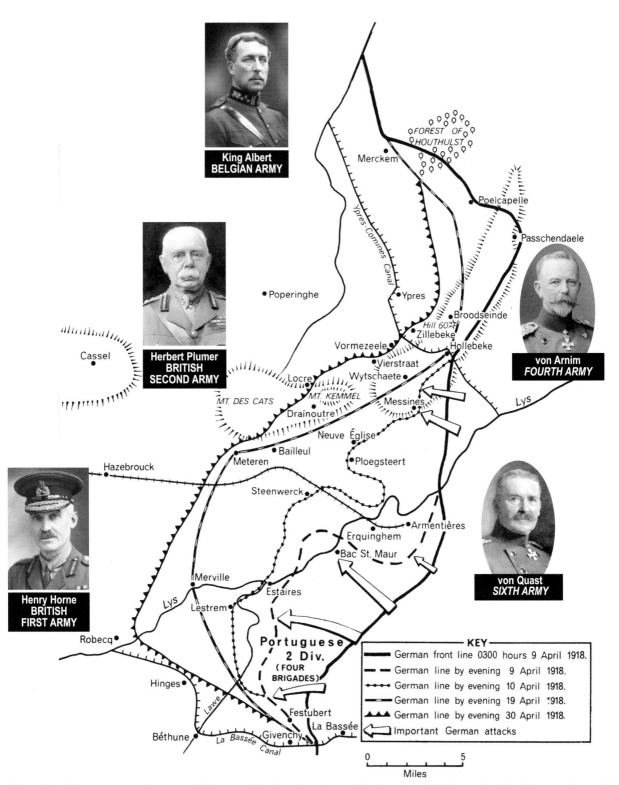

King Albert
BELGIAN ARMY

Herbert Plumer
BRITISH
SECOND ARMY

von Arnim
FOURTH ARMY

Henry Horne
BRITISH
FIRST ARMY

von Quast
SIXTH ARMY

FOREST OF HOUTHULST
Merckem
Poelcapelle
Passchendaele
Ypres-Comines Canal
Poperinghe
Ypres
Broodseinde
Hill 60
Zillebeke
Vormezeele
Hollebeke
Vierstraat
Cassel
Wytschaete
Locre
MT. KEMMEL
Messines
Lys
MT. DES CATS
Drainoutre
Neuve Église
Bailleul
Meteren
Ploegsteert
Hazebrouck
Steenwerck
Armentières
Erquinghem
Bac St. Maur
Merville
Lys
Estaires
Lestrem
Robecq
Hinges
Lawe
Portuguese
2 Div.
(FOUR
BRIGADES)
Festubert
Givenchy
La Bassée
Béthune
La Bassée Canal

KEY
——————— German front line 0300 hours 9 April 1918.
– – – – – German line by evening 9 April 1918.
•–•–•–• German line by evening 10 April 1918.
——□—— German line by evening 19 April 1918.
▲▲▲ German line by evening 30 April 1918.
⇦ Important German attacks

0   5
Miles

Operation Georgette was the second large scale offensive planned by Lundendorff. Its main objective was to reach the Channel ports of Dunkirk and Calais, thereby cutting supply routes to the British Expeditionary Force fighting in Belgium and France. It would become known as the Battle of the Lys and began on 9 April.

18GW184 Commander of the Sixth Army General Ferdinand von Quast and his Chief of Staff Lieutenant Colonel von Lentz at the time of the German attack on the British First Army front and the Portugese sector.

The main initial thrust of the German Sixth Army was against the Portuguese Expeditionary Corps: the CEP (*Corpo Expedicionário Português*). Germany declared war on Portugal in 1916 after the seizure of German merchant ships resulted in a declaration of war. The CEP was 65,000 strong.

18GW172 Portugese prisoners have their gas respirators collected by a guard.

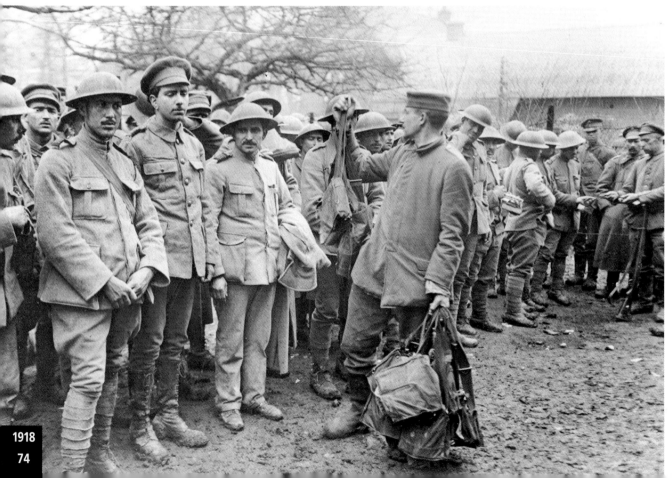

18GW171 Portugese positions had been overrun and many had fled; a large group of prisoners are seen here, awaiting removal to the rear.

18GW185 Portugese troops withdrawing before the onslaught – as were the British.

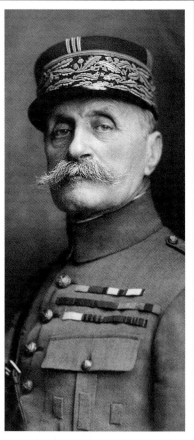

General Ferdinand Foch

With the German Spring offensive and threatened breakthrough, it became clear that a unified allied command was required. At a quickly convened conference held at Doullens on the 26 March, it was decided that General Foch would be given overall command of the Allied armies. Perhaps the representatives of British and French forces were impressed by a statement made at the conference by Foch:

I would fight without a break. I would fight in front of Amiens. I would fight in Amiens. I would fight behind Amiens. I would fight all the time. I would never surrender

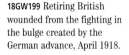
18GW199 Retiring British wounded from the fighting in the bulge created by the German advance, April 1918.

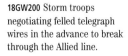
18GW200 Storm troops negotiating felled telegraph wires in the advance to break through the Allied line.

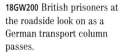
18GW200 British prisoners at the roadside look on as a German transport column passes.

There is no other course open to us but to fight it out. Every position must be held to the last man: there must be no retirement. With our backs to the wall and believing in the justice of our cause, each one of us must fight on to the end. The safety of our homes and the Freedom of mankind alike depend upon the conduct of each one of us at this critical moment.

(Signed) **D. Haig F.M.**
Commander-in-Chief
British Armies in France

General Headquarters
Tuesday, April 11th, 1918

18GW202 Walking wounded in Béthune from the fighting around Estaires during the Battle of the Lys, 9 April 1918. These men are from the 50th and 51st (Highland) Divisions and manage a smile for the camera.

18GW201 Men pulling back by lorries from the fighting 13 April 1918, during the Battle of the Lys.

18GW204 Men of the Warwickshires at Marquois, 13 April 1918.

18GW203 Men of the Warwickshires defending Robecq from a position on the edge of the local cemetery during the Battle of the Lys.

18GW206 Men of the 35th Division resting off the road to allow a retreating column to pass. These men of a fusilier battalion are marching to fill a gap in the line on the old Somme battlefield near Longueval. After three days' fighting the division was relieved by Australian divisions rushed from the north.

18GW207 Troops resting near Caestre on their way to the lines, 17 April 1918.

18GW205 A battery of Royal Artillery 18-pounders in action firing on the advancing Germans on 28 March 1918.

18GW208 British artillery in action to check the German advance near Albert, 26 March 1918.

18GW209 Firing shells at the enemy near Corbie, 1 April 1918.

18GW210 Soldiers of 93 Infantry Brigade who had been formed into a composite battalion made up of men from Durham, Leeds and Barnsley, marching to take up positions near Merris, 12 March 1918. Some of the men appear to be below average height and may be Bantams from the former 17th Battalion The Prince of Wales's Own West Yorkshire Regiment, who were amalgamated with the 15th Battalion (Leeds Pals) in 1917.

18GW211 Men of the Composite Battalion arriving to take up position. On 12 April the attacking Germans drove them back from the defensive position they had taken up on the railway embankment.

18GW214 Men of the South African Transvaal Scottish battalion take a roadside break during their withdrawal from action at Dernancourt to rest at Condas, 31 March 1918. When the Germans launched their attack on the Lys, the South Africans were flung into a counter attack at Messines and were pushed back off the ridge in the subsequent fighting, halting in their retreat at Vierstraat. In the fighting withdrawal the South African Brigade was destroyed as a fighting formation and the survivors from 1st, 2nd and 4th Regiments were merged into a composite battalion.

18GW212 A battery of hastely camouflaged British 18-pounders at Condas during the Battle of the Lys.

18GW213 British 6-inch Howitzers ranged on the advancing Germans on the edge of a wood near Boves, south-east of Amiens, 3 April 1918.

18GW215 Amiens was being shelled but this elderly French shopkeeper is still open for business for these Tommies.

18GW217 A roll call for men of the 1st Battalion, The Black Watch (Royal Highlanders) in front of their billets at Lapugnoy, near Béthune, April 1918. They were soon to be involved in the Battle of the Lys.

18GW218 Men of the 17th (Northern) Division move into reserve 17 March. After a five day retreat from the Flesquières Salient these men have fallen fast asleep.

18GW218 Part of the line near Meteren, where the line stabalized at the conclusion of the Battle of the Lys. A man of the 12th Royal Scots equipped with the latest model gas respirator.

18GW216 Men of the London Scottish, part of the 56th Division, marching back on 30 March after fighting a defensive action in the Arras sector.

18GW219 The vehicle shown is a French FT tank built by Renault and was used by Brigadier General Odlum, 11 Canadian Infantry Brigade, 4th Division. He used the vehicle for reconnaissance sorties that took him within range of enemy fire. It is halted on the Arras-Cambrai road. Canadian infantry are resting in the ditch.

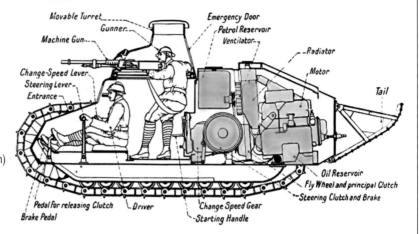

The Renault FT specifications

Total weight: 6.7 tons
Crew: 2 (commander/gunner, driver)
Engine: Renault 4 cyl petrol, 39 hp
Speed: 7 km/h (4.3 mph)
Range: 65 km (40.38 mi)
Armament
  Female: Hotchkiss 7.9 mm (0.32 in) machine gun
  Male: Puteaux SA 18 37 mm (1.45 in) gun
Armour: 22 mm (0.87 in)

Total production: 3,700 (France)

18GW223 A flimsy street barricade is flung together in Nesle near to the 20th Divisional headquarters.

18GW225 Men in a Lewis gun position, manned by soldiers of the Argyll and Sutherland Highlanders, await the swiftly advancing enemy.

18GW224 Battalion stretcher bearers at the head of the column lead the rest of the battalion away from the advancing Germans, 23 March 1918. These men are on their way from Péronne la Chapelette back to Maricourt.

18GW222 Following a sturdy resistance at Hermies on 26 March, the 17th Infantry Division was forced to retreat. Remnants of the division are seen here at Hénencourt, where they were reorganized to form V Corps Reserve.

18GW226 British infantry retreating in good order before the advancing Germans, passing tanks of the 2nd Battalion Tank Corps.

18GW227 British infantry advancing to support the defence of La Boisselle in March 1918.

18GW228 Men of the 1st Battalion Royal Highlanders (Black Watch) parade for roll call in front of their billets at Lapugnoy, near Béthune, 10 April 1918. Eight days later they were involved in heavy fighting along with three other battalions in trenches at Givenchy. Waves of attacking Germans were halted.

18GW229 Men of a Lewis gun team in a prepared position at Marquois, near St Veriant, 13 April 1918, during the Battle of the Lys.

18GW230 Warfare in open country meant that armoured cars could be used to good effect. This French armoured car had been sent to support British troops defending Meteren on 16 April 1918, when French divisions arrived under the command of General Robillot.

18GW231 German prisoners taken by men of the 31st Division or the 1st Australian Division during the desperate fighting around Meteren and Merris. Note the young man in civilian clothes being helped by two of the German prisoners. If he had been caught spying for the Germans he would have been later shot.

18GW570, 18GW569. Villers-Bretonneux, 24 April 1918, as viewed from the German lines and south-east; attacking A7V *Sturmpanzerwagen*. The Germans were attempting to force Allied troops out of the French village of Villers-Bretonneux, on their way to capture Amiens. The first ever battle between tanks took place when three British tanks attacked the A7Vs with mixed results.

Sturmpanzerwagen A7V

Crew consisted of up to seventeen other ranks and one officer: commander; driver, mechanic, mechanic/signaller, twelve infantrymen (six machine gunners, six loaders) and two artillerymen (main gunner and loader).

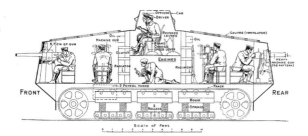

18GW567, 18GW568. French and British officers by the German A7V tank *Elfriede*, captured near Villers. Conditions inside these vehicles with eighteen men crowded round two centrally mounted Daimler 4-cylinder petrol engines, can be imagined. It was captured by A Coy, 1st Battalion Royal Tank Corps, at the Battle of Villers-Bretonneux, 24 April 1918.

Nursing sisters and RAMC orderlies dressing the wounds of British, French and German walking wounded at No. 29 Casualty Clearing Station at Gézaincourt on 27 April 1918. Three days later the battles of the Lys ended, General Ludendorff having abandoned any hope of obtaining a decisive decision there. He next turned his attention to the Ais. The total British casualties for the Battle of the Lys between 9 and 30 April were over 82,000 killed and wounded and nearly 32,000 missing.

Chapter Three: Salonika, Mesopotamia, Palestine

18GW232 Bulgarian infantry wearing German-style steel helmets using wire cutters on barbed wire entaglements.

17GW233 British troops and civilians fighting a fire caused by shelling in the town of Salonika.

THE SALONIKA FRONT 1915-1918

British and French troops arrived in Salonika as part of the Macedonia Front on 15 October 1915. They joined Greeks, Serbs and Russians; these in turn were joined by an Italian contingent in August 1916. In December 1916 the mixture of Allied troops attacked the Bulgarians and were stopped on a line running along the southern border of Serbia, east through Greece to the Aegean Sea. The line remained basically static until September 1918. The Allies formed a huge mixed camp of 600,000 men at Salonika, effectively described by the Germans as the 'greatest Allied internment camp of the entire war'. The Bulgarian army had proved itself capable, with some German stiffening, of holding its ground.

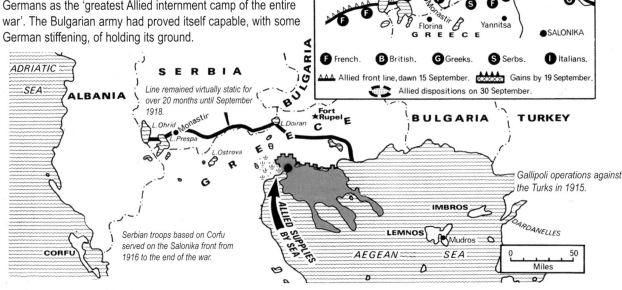

Allied final offensive in Macedonia in September 1918

0 — 50 Miles

SERBIA — Prizren, Skopje, Kumanovo, Gostivar, Veles, Debar, Gradsko, Krivolak, Berovo, Monastir, Florina, Yannitsa, SALONIKA — GREECE — ALBANIA — BULGARIA — Black Drin — Vardar — Crna — Bregalnica — Struma

F French. **B** British. **G** Greeks. **S** Serbs. **I** Italians.

▲▲▲ Allied front line, dawn 15 September. ▨▨▨ Gains by 19 September.

Allied dispositions on 30 September.

ADRIATIC SEA — ALBANIA — SERBIA — BULGARIA — TURKEY

Line remained virtually static for over 20 months until September 1918.

L.Ohrid — Monastir — L.Prespa — L.Ostrova — L.Doiran — Fort Rupel — GREECE — BULGARIA

Serbian troops based on Corfu served on the Salonika front from 1916 to the end of the war.

CORFU

ALLIED SUPPLIES BY SEA

Gallipoli operations against the Turks in 1915.

IMBROS — LEMNOS — Mudros — DARDANELLES — AEGEAN SEA

0 — 50 Miles

On 15 October 1915, two Bulgarian armies attacked, over-running Serbian positions and advancing towards Vranje. The Bulgarian forces occupied Kumanovo, Štip, and Skopje, and prevented the withdrawal of the Serbian army to the Greek border and Salonika. Marshal Putnik ordered a full Serbian retreat, southwards and westwards through Montenegro and into Albania.

18GW244, 18GW245, 18GW247. The Serbian army in full retreat, first from northern to southern Serbia and then across the mountains in Albania towards the Adriatic coast. Along the mountain route soldiers in the Serbian rearguard delayed the pursuers.

18GW236 Lieutenant General Sir George Milne, commander of the British in Salonika, with French commanders General Franchet d'Espèrey and General Henrys (right).

18GW249 A Serbian transport column in the Liouma region of Albania during the retreat to the Adriatic Sea coast, November-December 1915.

18GW248 Columns of Serbian troops in retreat in Kosovo. Note one of the soldiers struggling to walk on the left.

18GW250, 18GW251. Field Marshal Radomir Putnik, the Chief of the General Staff of the Serbian Army, was taken ill during the fighting and is seen in the retreat to the sea being carried by bearers across the bridge over the Drin River at Virzira, 17 January 1916. He died a year later in a French hospital.

18GW252 Conquering Turkish, German, Austro-Hungarian and Bulgarian soldiers in a Bucharest market sampling Romanian food.

As the Great War continued to spread, Romania joined the Triple Entente (Russia, Britain and France) in August 1916. After some initial successes, the Central Powers of Germany, Austro-Hungary, Bulgaria and Turkey, repulsed the Romanian attacks and within two months Romania had been overrun and occupied. The captured oil fields of Ploesti served the Central Powers until the end of the war in 1918. When Russia went out of the war in 1917 it left the remnants of the Romanian army completely surrounded by the enemy and it was forced to surrender in May 1918, signing the Treaty of Bucharest. Before the Great War ended, 10 November 1918, the Romanians unilaterally revoked the Treaty of Bucharest and declared war on the collapsing Central Powers and marched into Transylvania, Banat and Bucovina – which territories remain with Romania to the present day.

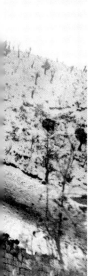

18GW246 Part of the Serbian army waiting for Allied ships to transport them to Corfu and other Greek islands, February 1916.

18GW255 Some Bulgarian reservists on mobilization (note the young boy dodging through their ranks).

18GW253 Anton Ludwig August von Mackensen, German Field Marshal. After Romania joined the war he was given command of a multi-national army and remained in Romania until the end of the war as military governor.

18GW254 Serbian infantry attacking Austro-Hungarian positions at Gantchevo.

18GW256 Romanian prisoners passing a wrecked limber near the capital, Bucharest: December 1916.

18GW256 Bulgarian reservists, transported by cattle trucks, arriving in Sofia.

18GW259 Nikola Zhekov, Commander in Chief of the Bulgarian army from 1915 to 1918.

18GW260 Emperor Karl I of Austria-Hungary taking salute from a commander of the Bulgarian Guard of Honour at Kyustendil during a trip with his empress to Sofia and Istanbul. From left to right saluting – Emperor Karl, Tsar Ferdinand I of Bulgaria, Crown Prince Boris of Bulgaria, 6 October 1915.

18GW258 Vasil Radoslavov, Prime Minister of Bulgaria; a firm supporter of the Central Powers during the Great War. He remained in office until June 1918 when it became ever more likely that the Allies would win and a more acceptable leader was required to achieve the best outcome for the nation in any peace talks and territory settlements.

After the Allied Gallipoli Campaign failed, Bulgaria sided with Germany. On 14 October 1915 Bulgaria and Serbia declared war on each other. Britain declared war on Bulgaria, followed by France,. Russia and Italy.

18GW261 Bulgarian infantry in trenches in Macedonia; this appears to be a battalion headquarters.

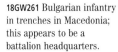

18GW263 The original press release photograph caption states: *The Balkan Crisis: strategical value of Uskub. The direct highway from Salonika into Serbia lies up the Vardar Valley, which is flanked by hills nearly the whole way from Uskub, rising often to over 1,000 feet on either side and this ancient Turkish town can only be approached by using the railway. Uskub is a point of great strategical importance, situated as it is at the great divide, from which the Vardar River flows south and the Morva River north to the Danube. Photograph is of Uskub showing the river in the foreground and commanding heights in the background.* A stamp on the back says TOPICAL PRESS AGENCY.

18GW264 A press release photograph by the French War Office: *One of the many guns on the Salonika front.*

18GW262 Another press release photograph: *Disembarking of French troops from the transporters in lighters to the quayside at the harbour of Salonika.*

18GW267, 18GW561. Russian troops marching to the front soon after arrival in Salonika; they have been issued with French Adrian pattern helmets.

18GW265 Italian soldiers arriving at Salonika in August 1916 adding to the confusion of allied nationalities operating in this theatre of the Great War.

18GW266 Serbian artillery in action on the Macedonian front. The Serbs had been re-equipped by the French and, no doubt driven by the need to free their homeland of invaders, proved to be the most effective troops available to the Allies among the numerous contingents arriving to fight in this theatre.

18GW237 The *Entente* in Macedonia. Left to right: a soldier from Indochina, a Frenchman, a Senegalese, an Englishman, a Russian, an Italian, a Serb, a Greek and an Indian.

18GW268 A British 18-pounder in action, November 1916. The British contingent faced the Bulgarian army on the right flank of the Allied line. The Bulgarians were turning out to be a formidable enemy.

18GW269 Bulgarian infantry in a forward trench on the Macedonian front. Often they were facing the British.

18GW270 Bulgarian prisoners of war being put to work cutting wood for shoring up trenches and stock piling firewood for use in the hundreds of camps fires.

18GW273 Original caption: *British mountain artillery in action on the Doiran Front in Macedonia. The screens over them are to prevent observation by enemy aeroplanes.*

18GW272 A British Official Photograph (press release issued by Central News) with the caption: *Giving the signal on the approach of the enemy's aircraft.* The bell was taken from a shelled church.

18GW234 British troops on the Salonica Front.

18GW274 Bulgarian infantry eating a hot meal in a front line trench. The original caption writer finds fault with the men's *'general air of carelessness – rifles flung on to the top of the parapet, very different from Western Front conditions'*; however, it may be noted that the rifles are laid out neatly ready for instant use should there be an attack (bolts uppermost). Also, none of the men have removed their equipment to eat their hot food. This scene depicts men ready for action should a need arise and anything but 'careless'. The infantry weapons appear to be Austria-Hungarian Mannlicher Model 1890 rifles, with a five round box magazine.

18GW279 French troops arriving in Salonika, raising a cloud of dust as they march along.

18GW275 A Greek regiment with its colours is setting out for the front. Because the nation was divided between the royalists, who favoured keeping out of the war, and the supporters of the Prime Minister, Greece had not officially joined in the fighting until June 1917.

18GW277 Eleftherios Venizelos, Prime Minister of Greece, brought the nation into the war on the side of the Allies. However, his pro-allied foreign policy brought him into direct conflict with the monarchy, causing the National Schism. The population was divided between the royalists and Venizelists; a struggle for power between the two groups would last for decades.

18GW278 Constantine I, King of the Hellenes.
His disagreement with Eleftherios Venizelos over whether Greece should enter the Great War contributed to the Greek nation being split. He favoured the Central Powers; he was married to Princess Sophia of Prussia her brother, was the German Kaiser. Blood ties between Sophia and the German Emperor caused the Triple Entente governments to view with suspicion King Constantine I and his neutrality in the conflict.

18GW280 A press release photograph by the French War Office with the caption: *Tommy's bathing place at Salonica. Amongst the hills on the Macedonian Front are one or two places that provide splendid bathing and Tommy Atkins is not slow to avail himself of it as here shown.*
An existing small dam has been heightened by the British to increase the depth of the water for swimming and bathing purposes.

18GW283 British draining the marshes in the continuing battle against the malaria bearing mosquito.

18GW285 A British soldier preparing for night duty is wearing a mosquito net against malaria.

18GW284 A padre bestows God's blessing on these British soldiers about to go into battle to kill some Bulgarians.

18GW286 After some days in the front line these British soldiers clean and repair their kit: the man on the left is using a pull-through to clean the barrel of his rifle.

18GW287 A British supply column halted on a road from Salonika to an inland front line position.

18GW281 A press release photograph with information on the back reading: *Official photograph from the Salonika Front. With the British in the trenches; a howitzer on the Salonika Front. Issued on behalf of the Press Bureau. Publication fee 10s 6d; please pay fee to Newspaper Illustrations Ltd. Passed by the Censor.* The gun appears to be highly maintained, spotless and polished.

18GW292 Gunners of the Royal Garrison Artillery manning their gun in Salonika.

18GW293 A British 60-pdr in action in September 1918. As on the Western Front, the Bulgarians constructed concrete casemates that could withstand numerous hits by large shells. The complaint was that there were far too few heavy guns to support the Salonika Expeditionary Force.

18GW288 A wounded man of the 10th Battalion, Black Watch being removed through a communication trench on the 'Birdcage' Line near Salonika. Note that they have not been issued with steel helmets at this time.

18GW291 Men of the Black Watch digging a drainage channel through the Daubratali Marshes to help destroy the area as a breeding ground for malaria carrying mosquitoes.

18GW304 Signallers of the Royal Garrison Artillery in Salonika relaying range corrections through a telephone line: the bombadier takes the message by telephone from a forward artillery spotter; a soldiers makes a note of the message and another man calls the corrections to the gun battery using a megaphone. Note the two unopened tins of corned beef, one each at the feet of the seated soldiers.

Lance Sergeant Harry Ashton

SHOT AT DAWN
for sake of example

During an attack on enemy positions on the 8 May 1917, twenty year old Lance Sergeant Harry Ashton missed the battalion's muster and departure into the line for the assault. The attack was a disaster; from the 11th (Service) Battalion, Cameronians (Scottish Rifles), thirteen were killed, 134 were wounded and 102 were missing. Total British casualties for the Division from 25 April to 9 May – the period of the assault against the Bulgarian positions – amounted to 12,000 killed, wounded and captured. The British had to call off all attacks at that time. Ashton was arrested and charged with desertion. He denied the charges; however, it was stated at his trial that he had made no attempt to re-join his unit, and indeed, had deliberately avoided doing so. Despite a previous good record (he had been wounded twice in fighting on the Western Front), he was shot at dawn on the morning of 8 July 1917.

Another man from a Scottish regiment had deserted the day before the same attack. Private Archibald Brown, 10th Battalion The Black Watch, who was already serving a suspended sentence of one year's hard labour for striking a superior officer; was shot by a firing squad from his battalion at 4.30 am, 1 June 1917. The controversial question must be: did these examples stiffen the resolve of the British Tommy, or embitter him?

18GW294 A Lewis gun team manning a post on a mountain slope. As the war drew to a close the number of Lewis guns per battalion had risen from 20 to 32.

18GW295 Royal Garrison Artillery troops firing their 2.75 inch mountain gun in Salonika, 1918.

18GW296 An episode during the fighting in Macedonia: a French patrol cautiously approaching a farm complex that may have been fortified by the Bulgarians. Three of their number can be seen spread out and in the open, walking towards the buildings, with their comrades ready to give covering fire.

18GW295 Royal Garrison Artillery troops firing a 2.75 inch mountain gun. The weapon is at full recoil and the bombadier appears to be knocked off balance. Under the leadership of French general Franchet d'Espèrey the Bulgarians were beaten back in September 1918.

18GW338, 18GW337. Salonika: A French field kitchen in a dugout and another being moved up a steep gradient by a team of six horses.

18GW339 A French 75 mm rapid firing gun rigged in the anti-aircraft position on a metal turntable. Some of the gun crew adopt an eyes-aloft stance for the camera while others in the crew show more interest in the camera, which would suggest that there is no real target in the offing.

18GW340 Spahis, French colonial cavalry from Morocco, on a parade ground in Salonika. These troops formed part of the Brigade Jouinot-Gambetta that captured Skopje on 29 September 1918. Note the movie camera man recording the event on celluloid.

18GW298 In September 1918, Franchet d'Espèrey, the new commander of a large army of Greeks, French, Serbs, British and Italians, mounted a successful offensive in Macedonia that defeated the Bulgarians, taking them out of the war.

18GW298 British officers examining a captured German Krupp 105 mm gun in a captured Bulgarian position, September 1918.

18GW297 Armées alliées en Orient – French watering their horses at a Macedonian stream.

18GW303 A Bulgarian machine gun detachment putting up a defence against the Allied offensive to drive them out of Greece.

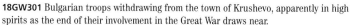
18GW301 Bulgarian troops withdrawing from the town of Krushevo, apparently in high spirits as the end of their involvement in the Great War draws near.

18GW290 A Bulgarian prisoner undergoing interrogation by French officers.

18GW282 A British Tommy with a group of French comrades at a captured ammunition dump, abandoned by withdrawing Bulgarian troops. The shells are German; Bulgaria had no sizable armaments industry and their weapons were supplied by the Central Powers.

18GW289 Following the surrender of their country to the Allies on 29 September 1918, these Bulgarian troops prepare for the rail journey home in open wagons.

18GW271 Three children of Monastir who have know little of peace in their short lives, growing up in two Balkan wars and then the great European war. They are fetching water for the soldiers; one of them has acquired a discarded steel helmet.

18GW313 A British monitor in action on the banks of the River Tigris.

Mesopotamia (between two rivers) – Tigris and Euphrates – was where the centre of the ancient world empire of Babylonia was located in 539 BC. The ruins of its capital city, Babylon, are still to be found 50 miles south of Baghdad. Towards the town of Basra and the Persian Gulf the land is largely desert, flat and floods during periods when the two rivers become swollen through seasonal snow melts in the mountains to the north. In the war years, due to the absence of good roads, transportation was along the rivers. The major city in the region was Baghdad, 570 miles upstream from the Gulf.

18GW307 Sir William R. Marshall, Commander in Chief of operations in Mesopotamia from November 1917 to the end of the war.

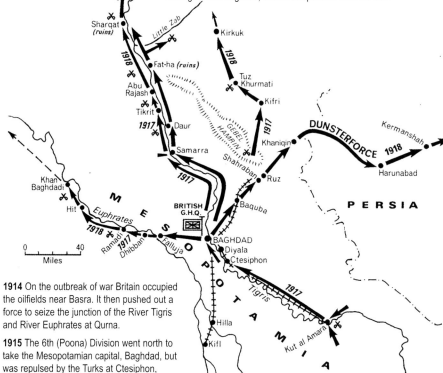

18GW308 Lionel Dunsterville, was appointed to lead an Allied force of 1,000 Australian, British, Canadian and New Zealand troops, accompanied by armoured cars, 350 km across Persia. His mission was to gather information, train and command local forces, and prevent the spread of German propaganda. Dunsterforce was to occupy the key oilfield and Caspian Sea port of Baku.

1914 On the outbreak of war Britain occupied the oilfields near Basra. It then pushed out a force to seize the junction of the River Tigris and River Euphrates at Qurna.

1915 The 6th (Poona) Division went north to take the Mesopotamian capital, Baghdad, but was repulsed by the Turks at Ctesiphon, retreating to Kut-al-Amara.

1916 The Turks pursued the British to Kut and surrounded them. All attempts to relieve Kut failed and the garrison surrendered on 29 April (see Volume 3).

1917 General Maude took command of the British army in Mesopotamia. He captured Baghdad in March 1917.

1918 Turkey signs Armistice (1 October 1918).

18GW314 Sir Stanley Maude, was appointed Commander in Chief after the British failure to relieve Kut al Amara. He directed his force in a steady series of victories: he recaptured Kut, took Baghad and advanced along both the Tigris and Euphrates. He died from cholera on 18 November 1917.

Mesopotamia campaign: cost to the British Empire
11,012 killed
3,985 died of wounds
12,678 died of sickness
13,492 missing and prisoners (9,000 at Kut)
51,836 wounded

18GW327 British troops marching towards Baghdad.

18GW318 Indian troops having recaptured Kut head towards Baghdad.

18GW329 Sir Stanley Maude. This extremely able British general issued a reassurance to the people of Baghdad.

People of Baghdad, remember for 26 generations you have suffered under strange tyrants who have ever endeavoured to set one Arab house against another in order that they might profit by your dissensions. This policy is abhorrent to Great Britain and her Allies, for there can be neither peace nor prosperity where there is enmity or misgovernment. Our armies do not come into your cities and lands as conquerors or enemies, but as liberators.

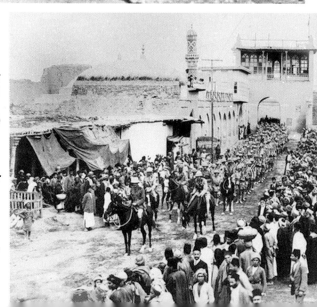

18GW326 Turkish troops retreating from Baghdad.

18GW317 Kâzım Karabekir, Turkish commander of Baghdad.

Karabekir ordered a general withdrawal and over 12,000 Turkish troops left Baghdad before the British arrived. When they entered the city on 11 March, there were still 9,000 Turkish soldiers remaining and they surrendered rather than resist.

The capture of Baghdad was a welcome anti climax for the British command, as General Maude had expected fierce resistance and he had been concerned that the defending commander, Kâzim Karabekir Pasha, would flood the plains on approaches to the city.

18GW324, 18GW330, 18GW320. Troops of the British 1st Division, 4th Battalion, Hampshire Regiment, entering the city of Baghdad on 12 March 1917, the day after its capture, passing crowds of curious inhabitants – for them just another invader.

18GW328 Turkish prisoners marching through a Baghdad street to captivity.

18GW323 Wounded Turks being tended at an Indian Army advanced dressing station.

18GW319 Troops of the Indian army in a Baghdad street.

18GW333 Sappers repair the Narin Kupri Bridge while British soldiers enjoy some bathing.

18GW335 British monitor HMS *Sedgefly*, with guns trained on a Turkish target, alongside the River Tigris. Clouds of smoke from the firing of the forward gun hangs over the ship.

18GW334 The deck of river monitor HMS *Sedgefly*, with the forward gun trained on a Turkish target, alongside the River Tigris. This type of river craft was a near indespensible weapon in the fighting in Mesopotamia. However, the river did not permit navigation much past Samarra, north of Baghdad.

18GW336 All four guns of a British artillery battery being towed by a caterpiller tractor alongside the Tigris. Good transport and an efficient supply system contributed to the defeat of the Turks in 1917 and 1918.

18GW311 Major General Lionel Dunsterville was ordered to occupy the key oil-field and port of Baku on the Caspian Sea. The special force – Dunsterforce – originally composed of 350 Australian, British, Canadian and New Zealand troops, accompanied by armoured cars, was to push 220 miles across Persia. It succeeded in fighting its way to Baku but the sea port, had to be abandoned on 14 September 1918 in the face of an onslaught by 14,000 Turkish troops, who took the city the next day. However, the Allies regained Baku within two months as a result of the Turkish armistice of 30 October 1918.

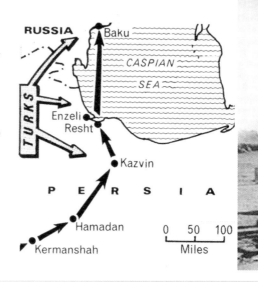

18GW342 Part of Dunsterforce: a repair team works on a British Rolls-Royce armoured car during the drive through Persia. An advanced party set out from Baghdad on 27 January 1918.

Weight	4.7 tonnes
Crew	3
Armour	12 mm
Armament	.303 Vickers mg
Engine	6 cylinder petrol 80 hp (60 kW)
Range	150 miles
Speed	45 mph

18GW343 A Dunsterforce convoy near Birkandi.

18GW344 14th (King's) Hussars, a part of Dunsterforce, resting on the road to the Caspian Sea port of Baku.

18GW310 No.9 Wireless Station returning from Zinjan, seen here on the summit of a pass near Sahneh, 26 October 1918. The Turks obtained an armistice on 30 October and hostilities ceased the next day.

On Christmas Day 1915 the Indian Government asked Australia for a pack wireless signal troop. One was sent in February. Immediately another troop was requested in order to establish an Australian and New Zealand signal squadron to operate in Mesopotamia. By May 1916 eighty wireless operators and sixty artificers, drivers and support troops sailed from Australia. These mobile signal stations became spread throughout the theatre of operations.

18GW322 Australian signallers listen in on an early Marconi Mk III crystal shortwave tuner set. This set could only receive, not send.

18GW309 An Australian and New Zealand wireless station (No.9 Station) with Dunsterforce crossing the Asadabad pass between Hamadan and Karmanshah, Persia, 1918.

18GW346 Dunsterforce on the march through Persia towards the prize of the oilfields.

18GW316 No.9 Wireless Station, marching with a reinforcement column on 18 September 1918, sent to support Dunsterforce at Baku, on the Caspian Sea, which was being threatened by the Turks.

18GW356 A 30 Squadron R.E.8 patrolling over the Baghdad-Caspian road in support of Dunsterforce.

18GW355 Dunsterforce camp at Hamadan.

18GW345 A Company of 7th Battalion, North Staffordshire Regiment, with Dunsterforce at Baladajar Station during the expedition to Baku, August 1918.

18GW348 Major General Dunsterville and his staff with an Armenian brigadier in what was known informally as the 'Hush-hush Push' to Baku and the Caspian Sea. Dunsterville was a friend of Rudyard Kipling and the writer based a hero for one of his stories, 'Chalky and Co', on the adventures of his friend who led a force from Baghdad through Kirmanshah to the inland sea. It was regarded at the time as one of the most romantic episodes of the war.

18GW347 A forest of oil derricks at Binagadi, north of the port of Baku on the Caspian Sea coast. The recently formed Bolshevik government had no control over the southern parts of the old Russian Czarist Empire and eager, interested parties made plans to seize the oil fields: White Russians, Turks, Germans and British focused on the area.

18GW350 A Dunsterforce expedition, with a Rolls Royce, armoured car coming under artillery fire from Turkish guns on the approaches to Baku.

18GW349 The port of Baku, on the Caspian Sea.

18GW351 Men of the 7th Battalion, the North Staffordshire Regiment advancing towards Baku and the oil fields.

18GW352 With Baku occupied, the British attempted to organize a fighting force from the Armenian militia. Dunsterforce men supervised training with Russian artillery pieces found at Baku.

18GW354 A Russian N.C.O. drills a group of Persian levies at Resht as a soldier from the Dunsterforce expedition looks on, hands on hips. Understandably, the Persians did not take kindly to being drilled under the authority of the British invaders; however, the caption assures us that their prejudice was *neutralised by the spread of confidence in British honesty and fair play.*

18GW357 Armenian troops in training to withstand the Turks at Baku. When Dunsterforce arrived at the town it was garrisoned by 3,000 Russians and 7,500 Armenians; however, when the Turks attacked they proved to be a weak force and provided little support to the British raiding party. The British were forced to withdraw.

18GW358 Turkish troops carrying an Islamic banner; the Turks could still cause the Allies problems but the British three-pronged drive north from Baghdad in the summer of 1918 finally brought Turkey to her knees.

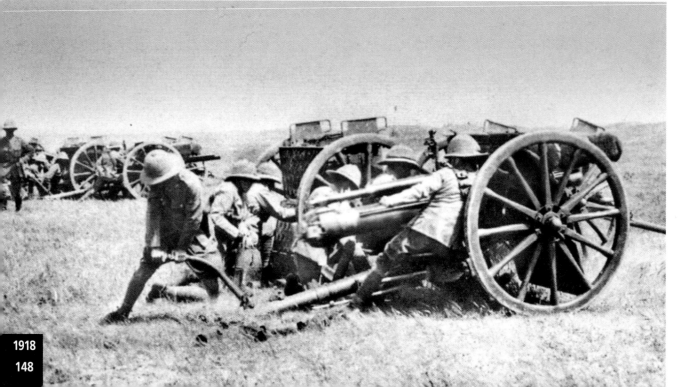

18GW361 A detachment of the 7th (Service) Battalion, Prince of Wales's (North Staffordshire Regiment), 39 Brigade, 13th (Western) Division, readying to advance against the Turkish occupied town of Kirkuk, May 1918.

18GW362 A battery of 18-pounders in action before the fortified town of Kirkuk, May 1918.

18GW363 Turks had given up the fight surrendering to British troops.

18GW364, 18GW360. The town of Kirkuk captured by the British (13th Division) and entered on 7 May 1918.

18GW365 Raising the Union Jack over the once Turkish headquarters of Kirkuk.

18GW359 A British soldier feeds his biscuits rations to wounded and starving Turkish prisoners.

18GW366, 18GW332. British soldiers of 38 Lancashire Brigade search surrendering Turkish soldiers captured after the action at Tuz Khurmati, 29 April 1918.

In contrast to many offensives during the Great War, the operations of General Allenby achieved decisive results at comparatively little cost. Allenby achieved this through the use of creeping barrages to cover set-piece infantry attacks to break a state of trench warfare and then use his mobile forces (cavalry, armoured cars and aircraft) to encircle the Ottoman armies' and cut off their lines of retreat. The irregular forces of T E Lawrence – Lawrence of Arabia – also played a part in the victory in Palestine.

18GW368 General Sir Edmund Allenby, commanding the British Empire's Egyptian Expeditionary Force (EEF).

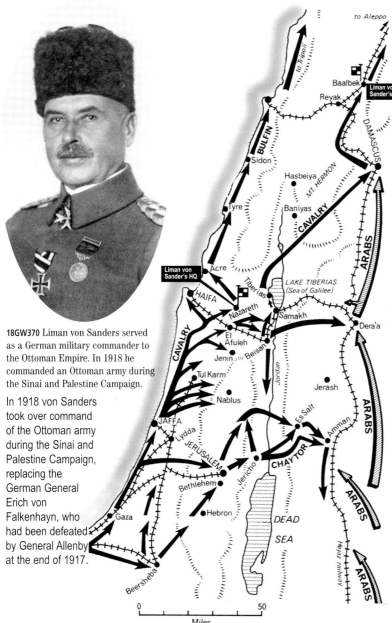

18GW370 Liman von Sanders served as a German military commander to the Ottoman Empire. In 1918 he commanded an Ottoman army during the Sinai and Palestine Campaign.

In 1918 von Sanders took over command of the Ottoman army during the Sinai and Palestine Campaign, replacing the German General Erich von Falkenhayn, who had been defeated by General Allenby at the end of 1917.

Lawrence was an archaeologist, military officer, diplomat and writer. He was renowned for his liaison role during the Sinai and Palestine Campaign and the Arab Revolt against the Turks. On 9 December, 1917, Allenby's forces entered Jerusalem. Lawrence was with him. In January 1918, Lawrence led an attack on the Turks at Tafila in which an entire battalion was destroyed. The British planned for a massive attack against the Turks on 19 September, 1918, and Lawrence was asked by Allenby to launch a diversionary attack on the Turks at an important rail junction at Deraa on the 17th. The British offensive was a great success and Prince Feisal was able to enter Damascus in triumph. On 31 October, 1918, an armistice was concluded with the Turks.

18GW369 Thomas Edward Lawrence.

Liman von Sanders was hampered by the decline in power of the Ottoman army. The force he commanded was only capable of holding defensive positions and wait for the British to attack. When General Allenby finally unleashed his army, the Ottoman forces were destroyed in a week of fighting. In the ensuring rout following the Battle of Megiddo, Liman was almost taken prisoner by British soldiers.

18GW388 On 11 December 1917, General Allenby, commander of the Egyptian Expeditionary Force, entered Jerusalem, two days after the Turkish forces occupying the city raised the white flag. Understanding the symbolic sensitivity of Jerusalem to religious adherents, he elected to make his entrance through the Jaffa Gate on foot. This was in contrast to Kaiser Wilhelm II, who, visiting the Holy Land in 1898, insisted on entering the Old City seated on a white horse.

18GW387 British generals on the Mount of Olives, 19 March 1918, enjoy the prize of the Holy City. Jerusalem was captured from forces of the Ottoman Empire by General Allenby in time for Christmas 1917.

18GW397 Friedrich Kress von Kressenstein, commander of the Turkish Eighth Army defending Gaza.

18GW403 Commander of the Turkish Fourth Army, Djemal Pasha, with his chief of staff to his left, behind the front in Palestine.

Two attempts by the Egyptian Expeditionary Force (EEF) to invade the south of Palestine near Gaza in March and April 1917 resulted in failure. The commanding generals, Archibald Murray and Charles Dobell, were replaced. The first battle had almost succeeded but the generals withdrew their forces due to concerns about the approaching nightfall and Ottoman reinforcements. This British defeat was followed a few weeks later by an even more emphatic defeat at the Second Battle of Gaza.

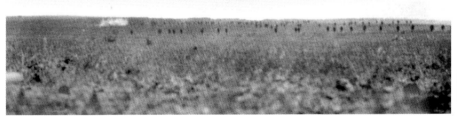

18GW402 Lieutenant General Sir Archibald Murray.

18GW398 The Second Battle of Gaza: the 1/5th Battalion, The Suffolk Regiment advancing from Sheikh Abbas on 19 April 1917.
18GW401 Survivors of the 1/11 Battalion, County of London Regiment, behind the Mansura Ridge, near Sheik Abbas, after the failed attack during the Second Battle of Gaza.

18GW400 Lieutenant General Sir Charles Macpherson Dobell.

18GW377 Major General Sir Edward Chaytor.

In 1917, Chaytor took command of the Australian and New Zealand Mounted Division. When taking part in the assault on Rafa he ignored Chetwode's order to withdraw and captured the town's main defensive position. In 1918 Chaytor's Force took Amman in Jordan and captured thousands of prisoners.

18GW378 The camp of A Squadron, 9th Australian Light Horse, in the Jordan Valley, near Jericho, 17 August 1918. The heat was so intense in this region during the summer that even the Arabs abandoned the region and dwelt in the hills. However, the holding of this ground was essential for the coming British autumn offensive.

18GW384 The town of Es Salt was garrisoned by German and Turkish troops and was the first town east of the Jordan to be attacked by the Australian Mounted Division.

18GW381 The approach to Es Salt littered with dead horses following the Australian cavalry charge in which the town was captured by the 8th Light Horse.

18GW379 Men of the 2/14th (County of London) Battalion The London Regiment (London Scottish), 60th London Division, entering Es Salt, April 1918.

18GW389 Lieutenant General Sir Edward Bulfin, commander of XXI Corps; he was a capable officer, leading his formation through the Ottoman defences at the Third Battle of Gaza, opening the way for the capture of Jerusalem. He later commanded the Corps in the overwhelming victory at the Battle of Megiddo in the final days of the war.

18GW390 A column of Australian Light Horse descending the hills and crossing the River Jordan, leading to the Auja bridgehead.

18GW391 The Jordan Valley, 28 August 1918. General Allenby inspecting officers and men of the Anzac Mounted Division, to whom he was about to present decorations.

18GW380 Turkish prisoners seated in one of the streets in Es Salt, May 1918. The town was taken by the 3rd Light Horse Brigade. The Turks counter-attacked in force and the Australian Light Horse had to withdraw.

18GW385 Men of the 5th Light Horse Brigade in a section of the bridgehead which had been established across the River Jordan on the eastern side. It had been put in place after the first raid on Amman and was retained throught the summer of 1918. Night attacks by the Turks failed to destroy this foothold and they suffered heavy casualties.

18GW412 British troops in defensive position adjust the settings on a 2-inch trench mortar, using what appears to be a Lee Enfield rifle bolt.

18GW413 British defences flanked by the Mediterranean Sea, manned in June 1918 by the 2nd Battalion Black Watch.

18GW414 A Royal Air Force S.E.5 of the 5th Wing, tasked with aerial cooperation and direct support to Allenby's ground formations. With an increased number of British aircraft in the Middle East, a Palestine Brigade was formed in October 1917.

18GW372, 18GW373. Battle of Sharon. men of 131 Brigade, 60th Division, escorting 1,200 prisoners taken by the Desert Mounted Corps, from Kerkur to Tul Keram, 22 September 1918.

18GW374 Battle of Sharon; railway station at Tul Keram taken by the 2/22nd Londons and 2/152nd Battalion, Punjabis, of 60th Division, 19 September 1918.

18GW375 Abandoned German or Turkish motor transport near Nablus on the Jerico road, captured by elements of the 10th (Irish) Division during their advance in 1918.

18GW395 Railway station at Semakh, on the southern edge of the Sea of Galilee. Here the 11th Light Horse Regiment encountered the enemy's rearguard, composed of Germans and Turks, at dawn on 25 September. After a mounted charge there was severe fighting and in and around the station buildings before the opposition was overcome.

18GW376 British soldiers clearing wrecked Turkish or German guns and transport from the Nablus-Jericho road where a retreating Turkish column was bombed and strafed by the Royal Air Force.

18GW371 British Mounted Yeomanry resting during the push through Palestine in 1918.

18GW392 Australian Light Horsemen and Turkish prisoners near Megiddo, Esdraelon Plain 22 September 1918. After a brief bombardment the infantry captured Turkish positions north of Jaffa. General Chauvel followed this by advancing with the 4th and 5th British Cavalry Divisions and the Australian Mounted Division. This mounted formation swept some forty miles behind the Turkish Seventh and Eighth Armies, cutting supply routes and communications,

18GW394 Turkish prisoners captured by the Anzac Mounted Division at Amman, 25 September 1918.

18GW392 Lieutenant General Sir Harry Chauvel, commanding the 4th and 5th British Cavalry Divisions and the Australian Mounted Division.

18GW405 General Erich von Falkenhayn, commanded the two Ottoman armies in Palestine with the rank of Mushir – Field Marshal. In February 1918 Falkenhayn became commander of the 10th Army in Belarus, where he witnessed the end of the war.

18GW404 General Erich von Falkenhayn, gives instructions to a Turkish mounted scout, Palestine, 1918.

18GW406 Turkish troops counter attacking on the shores of the Mediterranean Sea near Gaza. The British finally succeeded in driving the Turks out of Gaza in the Third Battle, which took place between 27 October and 7 November 1917. From then on into 1918 and the Armistice on 30 October 1918 the Turks continued to put up a fierce resistance.

18GW382 Brigadier General William Grant, commanded the 4th Australian Light Horse Brigade in 1917-1919 and temporarily commanded the Anzac Mounted Division in 1918. On 31 October 1917, his brigades led a successful cavalry charge at Beersheba.

18GW382 Australian Light Horse near Lake Tiberias (Sea of Galilee) – next objective, Damascus. The horses had suffered severely in the Jordan Valley and were in poor condition when the final offensive commenced.

18GW415 British transport camels near the town and plains of Megiddo, fifty-six miles north of Jerusalem, 22 September 1918. During the advance through Palastine supplies travelled close on the heels of the cavalry. Strategically located, overlooking the Plain of Esdraelon and major trade and military routes, Megiddo was important in the history of the nation of Israel and numerous decisive battles were fought there in biblical times.

18GW396 Emir Feisal I bin Hussein bin Ali al-Hashimi worked with the Allies during World War I in their conquest of Syria and the capture of Damascus in October 1918. Feisal became part of a new Arab government at Damascus after its capture. He sought a kingdom to rule and attempted to negotiate with the Turks on two occasions but was rebuffed.

18GW407, 18GW408 Emir Feisal and his tribesmen bodyguard. The Emir working with Colonel T E Lawrence as a united Arab force disrupted Turkish railway communications; drew troops and reinforcements away from the main battle fronts; pinned down forces in an effective guerilla warfare operation and at the same time avoided pitched battles with the Turks. They succeeded in cutting communication links with the north and Turkey on 17 September 1918.

18GW411 The Notts Royal Horse Artillery Battery (TF) in action at Kaukab, 29 September 1918 (looking from the horse lines to the gun position). After crossing the River Jordan south of Huleh, the Australian Mounted Division led the British advance on Damascus. At Kaukab, a few miles from Damascus, the Australians were stalled by a line of German machine gun posts. After heavy shelling by British guns the German postion was charged by the 4th and 12th Light Horse Regiments.

18GW410 Indian lancers riding into Damascus October 1918.

18GW386 Arab regulars under the command of Feisal captured the city of Damascus in October 1918. One of their tasks was to prevent looting; here Bedouin pillagers are being rounded up on the day of the city's capture.

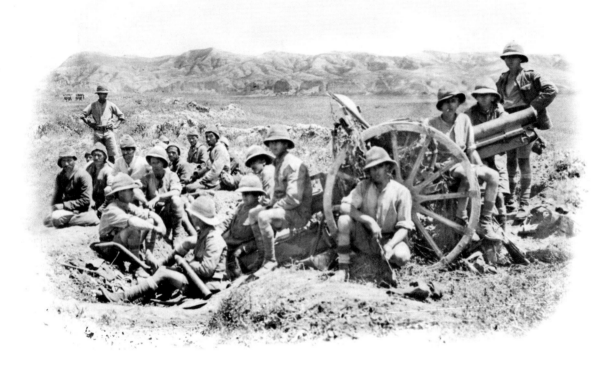

18GW416 British troops take over a Krupps 77mm field gun minutes after the Turkish surrender. The captured gun crew face the camera, along with their captors.

On the 30 October, 1918, aboard the British battleship HMS *Agamemnon*, anchored in the port of Mudros on the Aegean island of Lemnos, representatives of Great Britain and the Ottoman Empire signed an armistice marking the end of Ottoman participation in the Great War.

Chapter Four: **The Italian Front**

18GW435 Italian soldiers manhandling an 8 inch mortar into position somewhere on the Austrian front. Most of the fighting took place on the mountainous frontier region between the two countries. The Italian army was poorly equipped and was unable to move equipment and supplies quickly.

18GW434 The army of the Austro-Hungarian dual monarchy in the Great War was referred to as the Joint Imperial and Royal Army (*kaiserlich und königlich Armee*) or k.u.k. KuK and German troops are seen together with a 30.5 cm M11 *mörser* (mortar).

Prior to the First World War Italy had formed an alliance with the Central Powers of Germany and the Empire of Austria-Hungary; however, when war broke out in August 1914 Italy declared neutrality. Support of the Central Powers would not gain Italy the territories she covetted as they were Austrian possessions. Italy's leaders considered how to gain the most benefit from joining in the war, believing it would last only a few months. In 1915, Italy carried on secret negotiations with the Triple Entente (Britain, France, Russia) and signed the Treaty of London. By its terms, Italy would receive control over territory on its border with Austria-Hungary stretching from Trentino through the South Tyrol to Trieste, along with other territories that they had designs on. Italy declared war on 23 May 1915.

The front was along Italy's northern border, which was 400 miles long, mostly in the mountainous Italian Alps and along the Isonzo River. The Austrians owned the higher ground and after some initial Italian successes on the Isonzo front, the fighting became trench warfare with the Italian army taking the offensive and making no progress. Unlike the Western Front, trenches had to be dug on mountain slopes.

18GW436 Vittorio Emanuele III, king of Italy from 29 July 1900 until his abdication on 9 May 1946. Died 28 December 1947.

18GW417 Antonio Salandra, prime minister of Italy, 21 March 1914 – 18 June 1916. Died 9 December 1931.

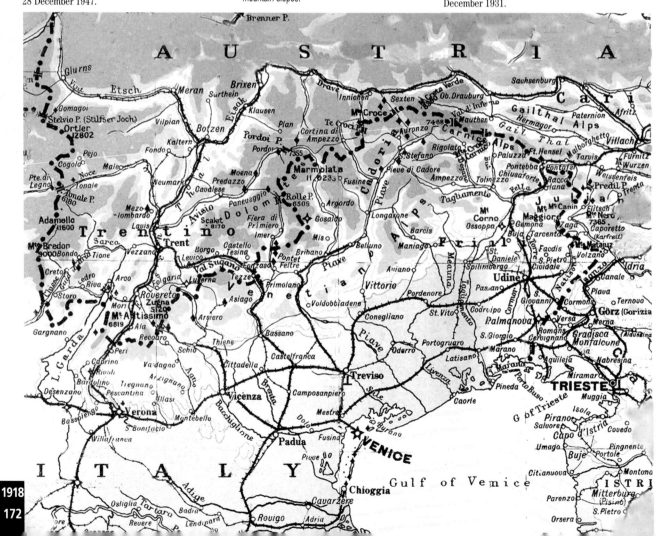

The Battleground
1915 – 1918

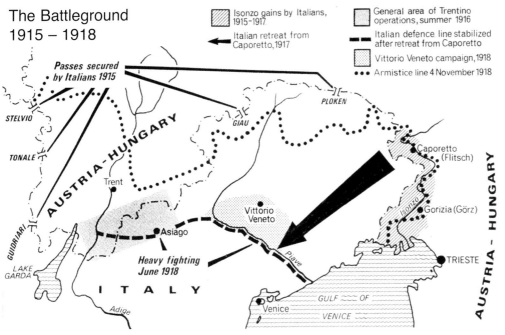

- ▨ Isonzo gains by Italians, 1915-1917
- ← Italian retreat from Caporetto, 1917
- ▧ General area of Trentino operations, summer 1916
- ▬▬ Italian defence line stabilized after retreat from Caporetto
- ▨ Vittorio Veneto campaign, 1918
- •••• Armistice line 4 November 1918

Passes secured by Italians 1915

STELVIO

TONALE

GUIDRIARI

LAKE GARDA

AUSTRIA-HUNGARY

Trent

Asiago

Heavy fighting June 1918

ITALY

Adige

GIAU

PLOKEN

Vittorio Veneto

Piave

Venice

GULF OF VENICE

Caporetto (Flitsch)

Isonzo

Gorizia (Görz)

TRIESTE

AUSTRIA - HUNGARY

18GW437 Italian Alpine troops. The Alpini regiments were never sent into battle as a whole, instead single companies and battalions were given specific passes, summits or ridges to guard and defend.

Between 1915 and 1917, Italian troops only advanced ten miles into Austrian territory, having launched eleven offensives along the River Isonzo, with heavy losses on both sides.

Following a failed attack by the Austrians in June 1918 the Allies, powered by the Italian army, launched an offensive in October 1918, known as the Battle of Vittorio Veneto, which led to the collapse of the Austro-Hungarian Empire and an armistice.

18GW438 Austrian mountain troops in the Isonzo area of the front.

18GW440 Dugouts, trenches and tunnels had to be carved out of the mountain sides. Austrian troops had to cope with the long periods of inactivity.

18GW439 An Austro-Hungarian machine gun team with their Schwarzlose M.07/12 This weapon was the standard machine gun of the KuK throughout the First World War and was used on all fronts. This team have their weapon trained on an Italian position on a mountain opposite; note the weapon is elevated to achieve maximum range – 3,000 yards.

18GW425 KuK gun crew operating a 30.5 cm mortar on the Italian front.

18GW442 Emperor Franz Josef I, Commander in Chief of the Austro-Hungarian forces. Died in November 1916, he came to the throne in 1848.

18GW441 An Austrian patrol high on the tree-clad mountain. Their resistance to the numerous Italian attacks was determined and largely effective until late in 1918.

18GW443 Emperor Charles I, succeeded his great uncle as commander in chief and ruled from November 1916 to 1918. In 1917 he opened secret negotiations with France. However, the Allies insisted on Austrian recognition of Italian claims to territory and Charles refused, which ended the peace moves.

18GW445 *Feldmarschall* Franz Conrad Graf von Hötzendorf.

18GW448 Two guns of a battery of 10.5 cm medium guns, manned by Austrians.

18GW446 A flamethrower being used by Austrian mountain troops against an Italian position situated below them.

Arz von Straußenburg's time as head of the KuK army saw more German control over Austro-Hungarian forces and reduced independence of action; but also a number of notable victories in the spring and summer of 1917, and the great victory over the Italians at Caporetto. Arz was responsible for planning the invasion of Italy during the summer of 1918. A clash of opinions between Arz and Conrad as to where the attack was to strike brought a compromise directed by the Emperor. The force was divided and attacked the Italians from two directions. This brought about a failure of the offensive at the Piave River in June 1918. By October Arz could see that defeat was inevitable and drew up plans for an orderly withdrawal should there be an armistice. On 3 November 1918 peace finally came when an armistice with Italy took place.

18GW444 *Generaloberst* Arthur, Freiherr Arz von Straußenburg.

18GW447 A German manufactured light trench mortar (9.15 cm *leichte Minenwerfer*) crewed by Austrians.

18GW456 Italian Alpini being inspected by Italian General Cordorna before the Battle for Monte Ortigara, June 1917.

18GW451 Standard Italian infantryman's weapon, the Mannlicher–Carcano M91 rifle. It was produced from 1892 to 1945. A version of the M91, fitted with a telescopic sight, was purchased by Lee Harvey Oswald and used to assassinate US President Kennedy in 1963.

18GW456 Italian Alpini wearing skis 1916.

18GW456 Italian Alpini manning a mountain gun in a position hacked out of solid rock, circa 1917.

18GW453 Italian Alpini hoisting a field gun to bring fire to bear on Austrian positions.

18GW450 Italian Alpini sliding across a mountain pass on a cable arrangement. The terrain made movement of men, artillery and supplies problamatic for both sides. He has an M91 rifle slung over his shoulder.

18GW452 Supplies could be brought only so far by mule before weapons, ammunition and food had to be winched up the mountain sides.

18GW463 An Austrian sentry keeps a watchful eye on the mountain opposite and the Italian positions.

18GW457 Italy's *Generalissimo* Luigi Cadorna, who was appointed as commander-in-chief in 1915. His constant attacks against the Austrians brought the Germans into this theatre of war to help their ally with the assault on the Italian positions on the River Isonzo. General Cardorna was criticized for his failure to prevent the disaster at Caporetto in October/November 1917. This unpopular commander was replaced, despite having rallied his forces on the River Piave.

18GW464 Before an attack: Italian infantry entering a sap on the Isonzo front.

The Eleven Isonzo Battles 1915-1917

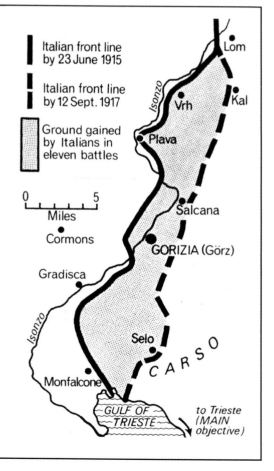

		Italian casualties	Austrian casualties	Remarks
1915				
First	23 June - 7 July	15,000	10,000	Italian gains
Second	18 July - 12 Aug	42,000	46,000	Italian gains
Third	18 Oct - 4 Nov	67,000	71,700	Italian gains
Fourth	10 Nov - 2 Dec	49,000		Italian gains
1916				
Fifth	11 - 15 March	2,700	2,000	Italian gains
Sixth	6 - 17 August	51,000	41,850	Italians gain 45 square miles
Seventh	14 - 17 Sept			
Eighth	10 - 12 Oct	75,500	63,000	Small Italian gains
Nineth	1 - 4 Nov			
1917				
Tenth	12 May - 5 June	132,000	52,300	Italian gains
Eleventh	17 Aug - 12 Sept	148,000	56,000	**Austria appeals to Germany for aid**

In April 1915 the Allies promised Italy the territory of the Austro-Hungarian Empire inhabited by ethnic Slovenes. Italian Field Marshal Luigi Cadorna, a proponent of the frontal assault, planned to break into the Slovenian plateau, taking Ljubljana and Trieste and threatening Vienna. The area between the northernmost part of the Adriatic Sea and the sources of the River Isonzo became the scene of successive battles. The Battle of Caporetto was a twelfth battle and was a German reinforced offensive which routed the Italians, causing them to retreat to the Piave river.

Italian front line by 23 June 1915

Italian front line by 12 Sept. 1917

Ground gained by Italians in eleven battles

0 5
Miles

Lom
Vrh
Kal
Plava
Cormons
Salcana
GORIZIA (Görz)
Gradisca
Selo
CARSO
Monfalcone
GULF OF TRIESTE
to Trieste (MAIN objective)
Isonzo

18GW462 An Alpini detachment of ski troops with Maxim machine guns gather for the camera.

18GW469 General Otto von Below arrived on the Italian Front in September 1917, commanding the Austro-German Fourteenth Army, which comprised seven German and ten Austro-Hungarian divisions in the Battle of Caporetto, his formations were able to break the Italian front line and rout the entire army. The battle was a demonstration of the effectiveness of the use of stormtroopers. Also poison gas employed by the Germans played a key role in the collapse of the Italian Second Army. A breakdown in German logistics brought the battle to a close on the line of the Piave River.

18GW471 German stormtroops, having newly arrived in Italy, practise their tactics before the assault on the Italian positions and the start of the Battle of Caporetto on 24 October 1917.

18GW478 Italian troops killed in a gas attack on the heights of Tolmin (Tolmein), November 1917.

18GW479 German Stormtroops attacking with hand grenades on the Isonzo front.

18GW474 Germans preparing gas projectors for firing.18 cm *Gaswerfer* (gas projector). A series of tubes to lob gas shells and triggered electrically were used at the start of the Battle of Caporetto. Hundreds of metal tubes were dug into a reverse slope and sent canisters containing chlorine-arsenic agent and diphosgene, smothering the Italian trenches in the valley in a dense cloud of poison gas. The Italian soldiers knew that their gas respirators would protect them for only approximately two hours, they began fleeing for their lives – over 500 were killed.

18GW480 A flamethrower being used to destroy an Italian strongpoint on the Isonzo

18GW473 General Luigi Capello, commander of the Italian Second Army. He was ill with fever and, realizing that his forces were ill-prepared for this attack, he requested permission to withdraw to the Tagliamento River, but was denied by Cadorna, who believed that the Italian army could resist the assault. After the defeat at Caporetto Capello was dismissed by Cadorna.

18GW483 Greatly helping the Germans and Austrians on the Isonzo front was the use of poison gas and flamethrowers.

18GW481 German troops in full marching order wearing all their equipment. The truck has on board Italian prisoners taken at the Battle of Caporetto; the action cost the Italians 165,000 men.

18GW482 German transport trying to keep up with the advancing army.

18GW484 Following the rout of the Italian army at Caporetto, the Germans and Austrians followed in pursuit. German artillery and supply wagons heading towards the new front line along the River Piave.

18GW485 Kaiser Wilhelm II reviewing the 2. Branderburgisches on 14 November 1917 following the successful Battle of Caporetto. The location is on Italian territory at Udine.

18GW468 Erwin Rommel after the Battle of Caporetto.

In the Italian campaign Erwin Rommel served as an *Oberleutnant* in the Wurttemberg Mountain Battalion, in which he was awarded the German highest order for bravery, the *Pour le Mérite*. During the Battle of Caporetto Rommel and his 150 men captured 81 guns and 9,000 men (including 150 officers), at the loss of six dead and thirty wounded. In yet another instance, convinced that they were surrounded by an entire German division, the 1st Italian Infantry Division – 10,000 men – surrendered to Rommel. He was promoted to *Hauptmann* (captain) and assigned to a staff position with XLIV Army Corps, where he served for the remainder of the Great War.

18GW467 Italian prisoners of war after the collapse of the front along the River Isonzo.

18GW460 From Caporetto to the River Piave, Italian troops in full retreat. The Italian Third Army had to march back on two roads which were crowded both night and day.

18GW466 Hastly dug Italian trenches along the Piave river. These men seem to be on the alert as one of their number has moved out towards a barricade to identify and challenge an approach on their position.

18GW458 Sixty miles from Caporetto Italian soldiers on the bank of the Piave. French and British divisions were rushed from the Western Front to assist their ally.

18GW470 Armando Diaz replaced Cadorna and organized the defence along the Piave River, which successfully halted the Austrian offensive. In the summer of 1918, he oversaw the victory in the Battle of the Piave River and, later that year, he led the Italian troops in the Battle of Vittorio Veneto, which ended the war on the Italian front.

18GW487 British artillery on the Mediterranean coast heading towards the Italian border.

18GW486 Italian General Diaz with Major General Babington, commander of the 23rd Division, one of the two British divisions in the Anglo-Italian Tenth Army (7th Division was the other). Following the defeat at Caporetto, British and French forces were sent to Italy to steady the situation.

18GW492 Men of the Royal Engineers, who had arrived in Italy by train, take to their bicycles to take them to their new base.

18GW488 French cavalry passing through Verona on its way to support the defence of Venetia.

18GW489 Rudolph Lambart, 10th Earl of Cavan. commanded the Tenth Army, which struck a decisive blow at the Battle of Vittorio Veneto, the action that sounded the final death knell of the Austro-Hungarian Army

18GW419 *Per favore, è questo il modo giusto per...* a British Military Policemen asking the way from a member of the Italian Carabinieri (likely with the aid of a guide book).

18GW492 Royal Engineers laying telegraph cables under the eyes of two Carabinieri.

18GW494, 18GW495. The original captions on this series of press release prints reads: *Outside a British billet; British soldiers among Italian peasantry.* Judging from their shoulder titles and cap badges, the soldiers appear to be men of the Army Service Corps. The first photograph shows curious locals turning up to greet the new arrivals and the next picture shows the children being befriended by the men.

18GW493 Men of the Royal Artillery, along with their horses, have arrived at a railway station somewhere in Italy.

18GW497 'Taylor and shoe-maker' reads the sign above these men of the Royal Engineers and the caption says: *Tailor and snob at work*. ('Snob' used to be slang for shoemaker.) Note the little helper.

18GW496 What must the children be thinking as this *un uomo in gonna* – this man in a skirt – plays them a tune on his bagpipes? The original caption for the press release simply states, *A village scene*.

18GW498 Original caption supplied: *An enemy aircraft that fell in our lines and burnt itself out with the two passengers. It fell in flames on the 24 December last, from a great height.*

18GW500, 18GW501. Original captions supplied: *British soldiers football team plays an Italian one. British side entering the field; the British eleven.*

18GW502, 18GW503. Original captions supplied: *British soldiers football team plays an Italian one. The Italian captain presents a bouquet to the British captain before the match. The General kicks off.*

18GW499 Original caption supplied: *British soldiers football team plays an Italian one. Distinguished visitors watching the play.*

18GW504, 18GW505. Original captions supplied: *Photograph taken on the British Italian front; scene in a small Royal Engineers Camp; returning from watering horses.*

18GW506, 18GW507. Original captions supplied: *Photograph taken on the British Italian front; Royal Engineers bridge building; scene during the dinner*

18GW508, 18GW509. Original captions supplied: *Photograph taken on the British Italian front; Royal Engineers returning from work; scene behind the front; R.E.s looking for wood*. Interesting that the men had to spend time scrounging for wood – presumably fence posts and stakes for re-use.

18GW510 Original caption supplied: *British Official Photographs from Italy; scene on the roadside. British Tommies make friends with some Italian gunners during a rest in a village on their way to the line.*

18GW511, 18GW512. Original captions supplied: *British Official Photograph from the Italian front; An artillery officer directing the fire of the battery according to directions from his F.O.O.* (Forward Observation Officer)*; one of the guns in action.* Note the soldier on the right with the field telephone receiving range corrections. The officer with the megaphone is also calling out range corrections.

18GW513 British trenches on the banks of the Piave river.

8GW420 Italian constructed trenches along the banks of the Piave; Barche, 1918.

18GW426 Overlooking the Piave, Captain Hardie, a war artist, photographed in late 1918 making sketches for his painting *British trenches on the edge of the Montello*.

18GW514 British trenches on the banks of the Piave River.

18GW421 British and Italian troops building a road block and machine gun position near Nogare, south of Covolo, winter 1917/1918.

18GW429 Arcade sector of the front: an Italian soldier helps a British officer and NCO become familiar with the terrain and Austrian positions.

18GW423 Italian troops repairing barbed wire defences on the banks of the Piave by the Montello. Montello is a bean-shaped hill in the province of Treviso, Veneto, northern Italy, which rises to 1,113 feet in elevation and dominates the area.

18GW427 View from the Montello overlooking critical roads from the Vidor-Covolo bridge.

18GW422 Bed of the Piave River showing channels, June 1918. The problems in attacking across terrain such as this can easily be imagined.

18GW428 British dugouts under construction at the western end of the Montello; Mount Grappa is in the background.

18GW515 Allied officers: Italian, French and British at a school for artillery instruction. The commandant is a British lieutenant colonel.

18GW430 British infantry returning from field training at one of General Headquarter Schools, Torreglia, summer 1918.

18GW516 Caption supplied: *British Official Photographs from Italy; A gunner of a battery spotting out hostile aeroplanes.*

18GW431 Burial at Padua municipal cemetery of three British soldiers killed during German air raids, December 1917.

18GW517 Austro-Hungarian *Sturmtruppen* at Holy Mass receive the blessing from the clergyman. By 1918 the Austro-Hungarian forces were war-weary and, like their enemies, needed to believe God would eventually favour their military endeavours. Most religious leaders on both sides laboured to keep war's fire stoked up. However, Pope Benedict XV attempted to mediate peace in 1916 and 1917, but both sides rejected his initiatives.

18GW524 Preparations were underway for a final offensive in the spring of 1918. Emperor Karl I of Austria-Hungary inspecting troops of a Bosnian regiment.

The American 332nd Infantry Regiment was sent to Italy in July 1918 in response to an urgent request from the Italian Government. They were to create the impression that a large force of Americans had reached the front and was preparing to enter the battle line of the Allies and take an active part in the fighting. It was hoped their appearance in that theatre of war would serve to demoralize the Austrians and boost Italian morale.

The Americans arrived in time to contribute to the Battle of Vittorio Veneto, the offensive that would finally break the Austro-Hungarian Empire and bring about an armistice some days before the war ended on the Western Front.

18GW432 Visit to the Italian front by American labour union leader, Samuel Gompers, in the summer of 1918; seen here with officers of the American 2/332nd Infantry. He was a staunch supporter of the war effort, attempting to avert strikes and boost morale.

18GW528 A British officer and six men with a Lewis gun holding a trench on an Italian mountainside.

Roana

AUSTRIAN POSITIONS

Concentration area for Austrian attack 14 June

LEINSTER TRENCH

MONMOUTHSHIRE TRENCH

OXFORDSHIRE TRENCH

Austrian supply line from Val d' Assa

FRONT LINE

18GW523 Asiago Plateau, the area of the Piave Line held by the British 48th (South Midlands) Division and attacked by two Austrian divisions, the 6th and 57th, on 15/16 June 1918. It bcame known as the 'Battle in the Woods and Clouds'.

18GW525, 18GW527, 18GW526, 18GW529. Austrian trained special assault battalians on the lines of the German *sturmtruppen*; these led the assault to attempt the final defeat of Italy. Men of the assault patrols are photographed prior to the attack – note the gas respirators.

After four years of war the fighting spirit of the Austrian army was seriously reduced and the men were suffering from shortage of rations and the effects of Spanish Influenza (a strain of flu which had reached pandemic status and would eventually kill 50 million formerly healthy individuals – before mysteriously disappearing in 1919). The final Austrian attack failed and on the night of 22/23 June, the exhausted Austrian divisions were withdrawn. The attackers lost 11,643 killed, 80,852 wounded and 25,547 captured. Now it would be the turn of the Allies.

18GW532 Austrian wounded await transportation to field hospitals. The Austro-Hungarian army was now a spent force.

18GW531 A column of captured Austrians being marched off to 'cages' led by a member of the Carabinieri – an Italian military policeman.

18GW533 Italian artillerymen loading a 6-inch tracked howitzer. The Italian army had been well provisioned and trained for the Vittorio Veneto final offensive under the generalship of Armando Diaz – 23 October, 1918.

18GW534 Italian Marines launch into the attack on the lower reaches of the Piave in support of their comrades, French, British and American allies.

18GW521 General Gaetano Giardino, commander of the Italian Fourth Army, who led the assault in the Battle of Vittorio Veneto.

Battle of Vittorio Veneto

Allied forces fielded 57 infantry divisions:

Fifty-one Italian divisions
Three British divisions (*23rd, 7th and 48th*)
Two French divisions (*23rd and 24th*)
One Czechoslovak division (*6th*)
One American Infantry Regiment (*332nd*)

Artillery pieces: **7,700**

The Austro-Hungarian army:
Forty-six infantry divisions
Six cavalry divisions

Artillery pieces: **6,030**

Both sides were afflicted by Spanish influenza and malaria. The Austrians were short of food and other essential supplies.

18GW518 Austrian prisoners of war taken during the Battle of Vittorio Veneto.

18GW520 American troops of the 332nd Infantry Regiment advance through Grave di Papadopoli during the latter stages of the offensive on the afternoon of October 31, 1918.

18GW521 Svetozar Boroevi, Austro-Hungarian field marshal. On the day of the Allied attack he ordered a counter-attack on the Italian bridgeheads over the River Piave, but his troops refused to obey orders.

18GW519 Italian and British troops passing abandoned Austro-Hungarian artillery on the Val d'Assa mountain road, 2 November 1918.

18GW535 In hot pursuit of the fleeing Austrians, these men of the Northamptonshire Yeomanry cross a stream during the Battle of Vittorio Veneto.

18GW459 Victorious Italian infantry marching towards their border with Austria. The Armistice of Villa Giusti finally stopped all fighting between Italy and Austria-Hungary in the Great War. The armistice was signed on 3 November 1918 in the Villa Giusti, outside Padua, in the Veneto, northern Italy, and took effect twenty-four hours later.

Italian soldiers of the elite Arditi Corps, the 'Caimans of the Piave' (alligators), brandishing their knives. They numbered around eighty and were trained to remain in the powerful currents of the Piave for hours. Carrying only a Sardinian knife – the resolza – and two hand grenades, they acted in a communication role between the west and east banks of the Piave.

Information used in this chapter was based on the following titles in the **Battleground Europe** series of guide books:
Asiago 15/16 June 1918, Battle in the Woods and Clouds by Francis MacKay
Touring the Italian Front – 1917-1919 by Francis MacKay

Chapter Five: **Battles of the Aisne and the Marne**

18GW170 The German army takes a leaf out of the British and French book of war and fields the A7V Panzer – in the streets of Roye, 21 March 1918.

18GW169 The Third Battle of the Aisne: French and British troops marching through Passy-sur-Marne, 29 May 1918.

The German surprise offensive, code named named *Blücher-Yorck*, was launched on 27 May 1918 and lasted until 6 June 1918. German commander, Erich Ludendorff, was confident that success at the River Aisne would lead the German armies to within striking distance of Paris. He believed that this would cause the Allies to move forces from Flanders to assist in the defence of the French capital, allowing the Germans to reopen their Flanders offensive with greater ease. Thus, the Aisne drive was to be a massive diversionary attack. Again, influencing the German planning was concern over the time when the American Expeditionary Forces would be finally employed against them in full force – a window of opportunity for the Germans was fast closing. The *Blücher-Yorck* offensive would become known as **The Third Battle of the Aisne.**

On the morning of 27 May 1918, the Germans began a bombardment of the Allied front lines with over 4,000 guns of all calibres. Because General Duchêne was loathe to abandon the Chemin des Dames ridge the British suffered heavy losses. The ridge had been captured at great cost the previous year and Duchêne had, in defiance of orders from the French Commander-in-Chief, ordered the defenders to stay in strength in the front trenches.

The bombardment was followed by a gas attack and then an assault by seventeen German divisions. Taken by surprise, the Allies were unable to hold the attackers and the German army advanced through a twenty-five mile gap torn open in the Allied lines. Reaching the Aisne in under six hours, the Germans smashed through eight Allied divisions. In three days the Germans captured 50,000 prisoners, 800 guns and were just thirty-five miles from their objective, Paris. However, the German armies were beset by supply problems, fatigue, lack of reserves and had suffered heavy casualties.

Crown Prince Wilhelm
German commander

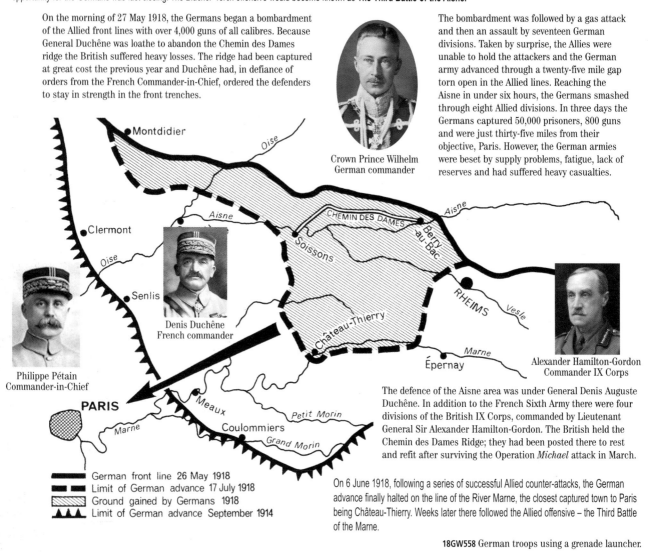

Philippe Pétain
Commander-in-Chief

Denis Duchêne
French commander

Alexander Hamilton-Gordon
Commander IX Corps

German front line 26 May 1918
Limit of German advance 17 July 1918
Ground gained by Germans 1918
Limit of German advance September 1914

The defence of the Aisne area was under General Denis Auguste Duchêne. In addition to the French Sixth Army there were four divisions of the British IX Corps, commanded by Lieutenant General Sir Alexander Hamilton-Gordon. The British held the Chemin des Dames Ridge; they had been posted there to rest and refit after surviving the Operation *Michael* attack in March.

On 6 June 1918, following a series of successful Allied counter-attacks, the German advance finally halted on the line of the River Marne, the closest captured town to Paris being Château-Thierry. Weeks later there followed the Allied offensive – the Third Battle of the Marne.

18GW558 German troops using a grenade launcher.

18GW543 German *Sturmtruppen* photographed leaving the lip of a crater during an attack.

18GW536 The southern bank of the River Aisne, 27 May 1918; soldiers of the Royal Worcestershire Regiment take up positions to repel advancing Germans.

18GW538 French infantry firing on advancing enemy during the Battle of the Aisne, June 1918.

18GW537 German infantry advancing past hastily dug trenches during the Battle of the Aisne river, June 1918.

18GW539 Chemin des Dames, May 1918, two German soldiers (one wearing a British sergeant's greatcoat) collecting useful items of equipment. Dead British and German soldiers lie in the trench.

18GW560 Men of the German Eighteenth Army attacking a position held by soldiers of the French Third Army in the Montdidier-Noyon area, June 1918.

18GW562 An aid post in a reserve line near Soissons early in June 1918. A wounded man is being carried on an improvised stretcher.

18GW559 Troops of a *Sturmbattaillon* after an attack south of Saint-Mihiel, spring 1918. The British Brodie helmet worn by one of the leading officers stands out in contrast to the 'coal-scuttle' *Stahlhelm*. As steel helmets were introduced to protect from shell schrapnel, the German helmet gave greater protection, but it was more uncomfortable to wear.

18GW563 Burning buildings in Soissons following its capture by the Germans, 28 May 1918. Immediately after its capture German troops were withdrawn from the town; the Germans were becoming critically short of all manner of goods and provisions and it was of concern to the German commanders that their men would find the stores and supply dumps irresistible. It had happened on previous occasions and focus on attack and continued fighting had become lost.

18GW565 German A7V tanks of the type that fought in the first tank-versus-tank action at Cachy, near Villers-Bretonneux, 24 April 1918.

18GW564 Inspection of troops by *Feldmarshall* Paul von Hindenburg, Chief of the German General Staff, during the initial successes of the *Kaiserschlact*, June 1918.

18GW571 German reserves have just crossed the Ailette and are resting before a further advance, May/June 1918.

18GW572 Blinded in a gas attack, two French walking wounded are escorted by their comrades and a British sergeant to a field hospital, July 1918.

18GW577 *Allies in battle and companions in distress* was the caption to this picture. The Official History of the Great War says of the enemy bombardment on 27 May 1918: '...*the continued effect on the guns, trench mortars and gas was indeed overwhelming. Casualties in the infantry had been very heavy, and most of the machine guns and artillery were out of action.*'

18GW573 French stretcher-bearers bringing in a British soldier wounded at Rethonvillers in the German offensive.

18GW573 A French Aid Post situated between Amiens and Montdidier, May/June 1918.

18GW581 A British 18-pdr gun and team are pulling back onto the road near Faverolles-sur-Ardre, having observed that their progress was barred by German troops in the process of occupying Faverolles-sur-Ardre.

18GW582 British troops on the reverse slope of a hill north of Courville, 29 May 1918. No time to dig even the most shallow of trenches, soldiers in retreat were subject to observation from the air and resulting artillery fire.

18GW579 The original caption reads: *They had been three days in retreat. The photograph was taken 29 May 1918, at Passy-sur-Marne. The Battle of the Aine had begun on 27 May and in less than three days the front line troops had fallen back between twnty and thirty miles. These men had been fighting near the junction of the Allied armies and the French and British troops are marching back together. A few miles further back the retreat came to an end on the Marne.*

18GW580 A battalion of British infantry crossing the Marne to the south bank. From the Germans launching their attack on the Chemin des Dames it took them four days to reach the River Marne, placing them just forty miles from Paris. However, the German attack was getting progressively weaker.

18GW584 Australian infantry of the 15th Battalion on the day of an action at Hamel, worn out and asleep under camouflage netting which had been found covering a German trench mortar.

18GW586 A British company in reserve: an NCO writes a message under the watchful eyes of officers and a runner stands ready to deliver it. Note the vase of cut wild flowers on the table.

18GW585 A German outpost captured in a daylight attack on 9 July and manned by Australian infantry – they are setting up a Stokes mortar. On 4 July the Australians launched a very successful limited attack at Le Hamel.

18GW583 Hitching a ride on a tractor-drawn 8-inch howitzer, these retreating troops appear cheerful for the camera. This is a road near Fismes, which had been about fifteen miles behind the front line before the German attack.

18GW599 A battery of French 75s in position near Montdidier during the Battle of Amiens in August 1918.

18GW598 Original caption reads: *on 15 August 1918, a solemn Mass was held in Amiens Cathedral to commemorate the liberation of the city from the menace of the German guns. Our illustration shows the officiating clergy, one of them an Army chaplain, and the congregation in the chancel on that occasion.* Note the sand bagged interior.

18GW597 Field Marshal Sir Douglas Haig inspecting a Canadian battalion.

18GW595 The German Kaiser, Wilhelm II, handing out decorations for bravery after the successful *Kaiserschlacht* advance of 1918.

18GW587 French cavalry working with British infantry as the German offensive lost its impetus.

18GW575 French infantry moving forward passes a British band sitting at the roadside. Strength was gathering for a counter attack.

Germany produced an amazing artillery weapon in the final year of the war. The weapon was a 15-inch naval cannon fitted with an inner tube. It threw a 9.1 inch shell the 75 miles to hit Paris; one of three of these guns was located near Crépy en Laonnois, in the forest of St Gobain. The threat to their capital city had to be removed as a matter of some urgency for the French.

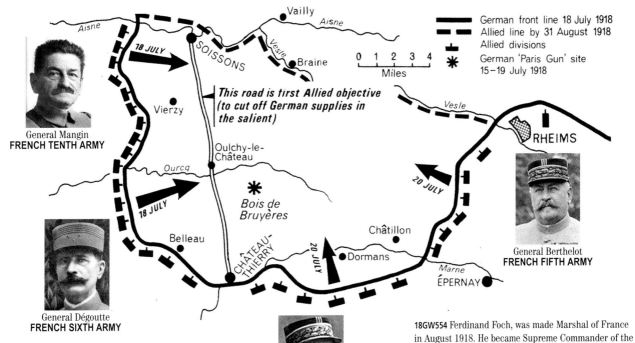

▬▬▬	German front line 18 July 1918
▬ ▬ ▬	Allied line by 31 August 1918
⊏	Allied divisions
✱	German 'Paris Gun' site 15–19 July 1918

0 1 2 3 4 Miles

This road is first Allied objective (to cut off German supplies in the salient)

General Mangin
FRENCH TENTH ARMY

General Dégoutte
FRENCH SIXTH ARMY

General de Mitry
FRENCH NINTH ARMY

General Berthelot
FRENCH FIFTH ARMY

18GW554 Ferdinand Foch, was made Marshal of France in August 1918. He became Supreme Commander of the Allied forces in France in March and led the Allies to final victory in November 1918.

The German failure to break through, or to defeat the Allied armies gave Ferdinand Foch, the Allied Supreme Commander, the opportunity to proceed with the planned major counteroffensive on 18 July; twenty-four French divisions, including the American 92nd and 93rd Infantry Divisions under French command, joined by other Allied troops, including eight large American divisions under American control and 350 tanks, attacked the newly created German salient. The engagement marked the beginning of a German withdrawal that was never reversed. In September 1918 nine American divisions (about 243,000 men) joined four French divisions to push the Germans from the St. Mihiel Salient.

18GW588 Men of the Royal Artillery watch as their comrades march towards positions for an offensive on the Marne.

18GW555 French troops under General Gouraud driving back the Germans near the River Marne 1918, seen here with their machine guns amongst the ruins of a church near the Marne.

18GW188 One of three 1918 production German artillery weapons, these were 15-inch naval cannons fitted with an inner tube. They could hurl a 9-inch shell on a trajectory that reached over twenty miles high. The 'Paris' gun, which carried out a constant bombarment from 23 March to 9 August, was nicknamed 'Wilhelm's Gun' and was located near Crépy en Laonnois in the Forest of St Gobain and could bombard Paris seventy-five miles away.

18GW590, 18GW591, 18GW592, 18GW593, 18GW594. French soldiers advancing near Soissons, July 1918. The terrain has not been destroyed by heavy shelling, apart from a line of shell torn trees marking the German trench lines. The scene in the captured trench shows French stretcher bearers given first aid to wounded German prisoners.

1918

247

18GW601 German *Sturmtruppen* ready to go into action during the Marne offensive in July 1918. They were approaching the end of their offensive spirit: a break through and rout of the allied armies had not occured as expected; resistance had stiffened; supplies, reserves and replacements were not getting through in sufficient amounts and the Americans were taking the field in ever growing numbers.

18GW602 Soldiers of the American Expeditionary Forces, 33rd Infantry Division, at Corbie, 3 July 1918, the day before they went into action with the Australian Corps at Hamel. Their commander, General Pershing, had been reluctant to permit their being employed in this manner but had allowed four companies to be incorporated in the Australian assault battalions. The attack was a success although, out of the one thousand Americans who went into action, six officers and 128 other ranks became casualties.

18GW600 Photograph taken on 5 July 1918 near Pear Trench, Hamel – German dead.

18GW596 Utterly exhausted Germans, recently captured by the French, sleeping where they had collapsed on building materials for the prisoner of war camp being constructed nearby.

Chapter Six: Americans
at Cantigny, Château-Thierry, St Mihiel, Meuse-Argonne

18GW603 The United States declared war on Germany 6 April 1917, by May 1918, 500,000 had arrived in France and by mid July 1918 the number had increased to over one million men.

18GW604 German troops on a road within the salient they had created by their offensive on the Aisne; wounded and artillery are withdrawing, passing advancing reserves.

18GW618 United States Infantry arriving at the French seaport of Brest.

18GW619 Marching to camp on French soil; it was planned that there would follow six to eight month's further training on how to fight in a twentieth century European war.

18GW617 Major General John J. Pershing's welcome on British soil, 8 June 1917: he arrived at Liverpool, where a guard of honour was formed by soldiers of the Welsh Fusiliers. The original caption, written by an American reporter, noted that the soldiers were boys. Actually at that time they were all at least eighteen – early days of compulsory conscription. The British were beginning to suffer a dearth in grown men; the Americans had arrived in the nick of time. General Pitcairn Campbell is the accompanying officer representing the British War Office.

18GW608 Commander of the American Expeditionary Force, General Pershing at his General Headquarters in Chaumont, France, October 1918.

18GW611 Throughout 1918 a flow of men and materials from the United States continued to arrive at European ports.

18GW613 Officers and NCOs of a Highland regiment oversee the training of the new arrivals. The American issue Springfield rifles have been stacked and the GIs practice live firing with the British Short Lee Enfield.

18GW609 American troops learning to operate the Hotchkiss M1909 Benét–Mercié light machine gun. This has a 30-round strip magazine.

18GW610 An American soldier being trained on the French Fusil Mitrailleur Modele 1915 CSRG by a Chasseurs Alpins.

American divisions arriving in europe were sent to training camps for a period of six to eight weeks where men could become acclimatized to the atmosphere of war. In the words of General Pershing, their commander:

This war has developed special features which involve special phases of training but the fundamental ideas enunciated in our Drill Regulations and other service manuals remain the guide for both officers and soldiers. The rifle and bayonet are the principal weapons of of the infantry soldier. He will be trained to a high degree of skill as a marksman both on the target range and in field firing. An aggressive spirit must be developed until the soldier feels, as a bayonet fighter, invincible in battle.

18GW612 Sergeant Harris, who formerly served with the US 1st Regiment, New Mexico National Guard, and now a weapons instructor in a British Highland regiment, instructs American troops on the workings of a British Vickers machine gun.

18GW627 French troops demonstrate how to fire a rifle grenade.

18GW621 A French officer showing how to fit the all-important gas respirator.

18GW628 Using their Remingtons on the firing range to identify the marksmen among the them.

18GW626 Newly formed US Army medical staff enjoying some relaxation. The American Expeditionary Force did not have a medical corps in 1917. The medical corps that came into existence copied the British medical system which was arranged military with stretcher-bearers being the first to render first aid to the wounded then carrying them from the trenches to aid posts. The first aid treatment these medics gave often saved lives.

18GW661 A Lewis gun team in training, summer of 1918. The Lewis gun was invented by US Army colonel Isaac Newton Lewis in 1911, but was not initially adopted by the US military. In 1914, Birmingham Small Arms Company (BSA) purchased a licence to manufacture the Lewis machine gun in England.

Legend:
→ American attacks
- - Front line 18 July
— Armistice line 11 November

0 — 50 Miles

AMERICAN TROOPS IN ACTION on the WESTERN FRONT 1918
American soldiers went into action in Europe in 1918 in six areas of the front: the above map shows the various regions where they were employed. The first offensive action by AEF units serving under non-American command was 1,000 men (four companies from the 33d Division AEF) with the Australian Corps during the Battle of Hamel, Somme region, on 4 July 1918.

18GW632 Soldiers of the 101st Infantry Regiment, 26th Infantry Division, in the trenches at Neufchateau.

18GW629 Men of the 1st US Infantry Division in the trenches in the Toul sector, where the AEF went into the line for the first time in the winter of 1917.

18GW633 A worker with the Y.M.C.A. serving hot chocolate to Yanks and a Poilu in the front line. The Young Men's Christian Association distributed vast quantities of refreshments to troops on the move: one centre at a railway siding at Étaples served more than 200,000 cups of cocoa each month.

18GW630 Americans of the 18th Regiment, 1st Infantry Division in a communication trench at Ansauville, November 1917, peer in the direction of the enemy for the first time.

18GW631 The American manned field gun that fired the first shot at the Germans on behalf of the United States on 23 October 1917. It was crewed by men of Battery C, 6th Field Artillery, 1st Infantry Division

18GW635 A Roman Catholic US Army chaplain holding forth at a service in a town well behind the lines. His opposite number in the German army would be doing the same, encouraging his listeners to destroy the enemy for the sake of liberty and justice.

18GW716 Three American officers try firing the French designed 37 mm 1916 fast firing cannon. It was intended to destroy enemy machine gun posts, (a job more effectively handled by mortars).

18GW636 *Here lie the first soldiers of the United States to fall on the soil of France for liberty and justice.* The inscription on the board for three graves named the men as Corporal James D Gresham and Privates Thomas F Enright and Merle D Hay, 16th Infantry Regiment, 1st Infantry Division. They lost their lives on the night of 3 December 1917 when a German raiding party attacked the American-held trenches near Bures, Bathelemont.

18GW634 American troops rehearsing for a German gas attack try out their respirators.

264

18GW637 The first German prisoner to be captured by the 26th Infantry Division is paraded with pride before the camera by Sergeant John Letzing, 104th Infantry Regiment. The prisoners's name was Robert Froehlich, taken on 17 February 1918.

18GW638 Miss Gladys McIntyre of the Salvation Army serving doughnuts to men of the 26th Infantry Division.

18GW640 American troops and Poilus sharing a couple of bottles of wine, drink a toast to victory behind the front line.

18GW639 Men of the 167th Infantry Regiment (4th Alabama) eating chow in the front line trenches..

18GW641, 18GW642. A medical officer working on some early American casualties at a dressing station near the village of Bertrichamps, 26 April 1918.

18GW645 Men of the 165th Infantry Regiment (69th New York National Guard) about to move up to the front line at Croismare, 2 March 1918. Note the French guides waiting to lead them in.

18GW643 Lieutenant Colonel George Florence and Major R G Allen, along with members of the staff of the 166th Infantry Regiment, leaving the HQ dugout for inspection of the trenches at Blemery.

18GW646, 18GW647. American infantryman in heavy marching order, front and rear.

18GW644 First of many more to follow: Private Dyer J Bird, 166th Infantry Regiment at Domjevin, 3 March 1918. Private Bird was killed while manning a listening post when a German raiding party attacked it. The flag-draped coffin was certainly a luxury to be rarely repeated, but the image on this occasion would have been provided to give a measure of comfort for home consumption.

18GW648 A 42nd Infantry Division outpost in the woods at Parroy, east of Luneville, 5 March 1918. The 42nd Division was serving with the French VII Corps. Shortly after this picture was taken a German shell destroyed the position.

18GW649 Men of the 167th Infantry Regiment resting behind the lines near Neuviller, 10 May 1918.

18GW653 The original caption: *Men of the 165th Infantry throwing handgrenades at 'Heinie' near Brouville, 16 April 1918*; however, it appears to be live grenade throwing practise, judging by the lack of cover taken by these men.

18GW651 Men of the 26th Field Signal Battalion engaged in line laying and telephone installation in the Soissons sector, 12 March 1918.

18GW652 Intelligence personnel attached to the 168th Infantry Regiment at Badonviller, trying on specially designed snipers' camouflage clothing developed by the British.

18GW650 German speaking Intelligence officers with the 42nd Infantry Division interrogating three prisoners captured at Baccarat.

18GW654, 18GW655, 18GW656, 18GW657. A series of photographs taken 17/18 March 1918, showing French and American soldiers on a combined bombing sortie. The US soldiers are carrying sacks of grenades and the captions read: *In a sector near Badonviller American and French officers cut the barbed wire preparatory to a raid; Iowans of the 168th Infantry Regiment advance into No Man's Land through the path through the wire; patrol under Lieutenant Curry going out into No Man's Land.*

18GW658 Before going into battle men of the 101st Infantry Regiment attend Holy Communion. A solemn occasion to take emblems of the body and blood of the Christ, the King of Peace.

18GW614 American supply lorries and carts on the way to the front line 1918, pause in their journey for a photographer.

18GW672 French school children of Soulosse take time from their lessons to watch the advance unit of the American 101st Division Ammunition train pass through their town, 10 April 1918.

18GW678 German *Sturmtruppen* leading the attack with handgrenades bursting through the cover of a smoke screen.

18GW679 The French village of Seicheprey from the air where Amercan soldiers experienced their first real taste of modern warfare when the Germans attacked the village on the 20 April 1918 during their 'Michael' Offensive .

The French village of Seicheprey was the scene of the first serious encounter between the Americans and the Germans. The German assaulting troops amounted to 2,800 men, which included in the lead a battalion of specially trained Sturmtruppen. The attack was met by elements of the 102nd Infantry Regiment under the command of Colonel 'Gatling Gun Parker'. The assaulting Germans lost 1,851 men and the defending Americans 1,064.

We have passed successfully the most terrific test ever imposed on American troops in France and we have proved that American militia can be relied upon to fight to the death under orders.
Colonel 'Gatling Gun Parker'
Commanding 102nd Infantry Regiment

18GW680 John Henry Parker, 'Gatling Gun Parker', commanding 102nd Infantry Regiment. He had been in charge of a Gatling gun detachment of the US Army's Fifth Army Corps to devastating effect in Cuba in the Spanish-American War of 1898, hench the nickname.

18GW676 Robert Lee Bullard,
commanding the US First Division.

THE VILLAGE OF CANTIGNY was situated on high ground surrounded by woods, making it an ideal observation post for German artillery. On the 28 May 1918 men of the American Expeditionary Force launched their first attack of the war on the village with 3,564 men of the 28th Infantry Regiment (Colonel Hansen Ely, commanding) plus two companies of the 18th Infantry Regiment, three machine gun companies and a company of engineers. The French provided air cover, 368 heavy artillery pieces, trench mortars, tanks and flamethrowers. The French Schneider tanks were from the French 5th Tank Battalion. The tanks were to eliminate German machine gun positions. With this massive support, and advancing on schedule behind a creeping artillery barrage, the 28th Infantry Regiment took the village in 30 minutes. It then continued on to its final objective, about half a kilometre beyond the village.

18GW677 Oskar von Hutier commanding
the German Eighteenth Army.

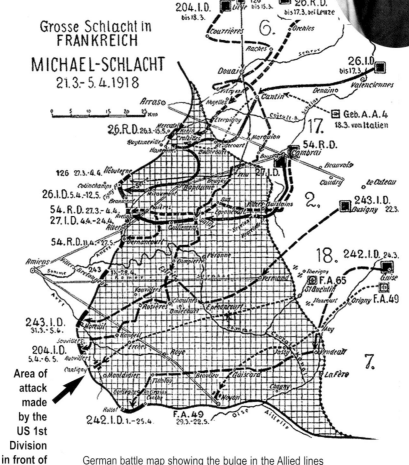

18GW673 Colonel Hanson
Ely, commanding 28th
Infantry Regiment.

Area of attack made by the US 1st Division in front of Cantigny, 28 May 1918

German battle map showing the bulge in the Allied lines created by their Michael Offensive in March/April 1918.

18GW682 American artillery of the 1st Division. A two hour bombardment took place prior to the attack on the German lines at Cantigny.

18GW669 American infantry laying down a smoke screen by using rifle-launched grenades.

18GW668, 18GW664, 18GW675. American soldiers of the 28th Infantry Regiment readying themselves for their first agressive action of the war – an attack on the high ground around the village of Cantigny. They would be supported by French artillery, aircraft, flamethrower units and some Schneider tanks.

18GW659, 18GW660, 18GW670. At 06:45 (H Hour), 28 May 1918, American Soldiers of the 28th Infantry Regiment left their jump-off trenches following an hour-long artillery preparation. A rolling barrage, advancing 100 metres every two minutes, was calculated to give the attacking troops time to keep up with it. Success at Cantigny assured the French that American divisions could be entrusted in the line against the German offensive to take Paris. The Americans took the village in thirty minutes, then carried on to their final objective half a kilometre beyond the village. The victory at Cantigny was followed by attacks at Château-Thierry and Belleau Wood in the first half of June.

18GW684 Aerial photograph taken of the village of Cantigny during the fighting to recapture it from the Germans, 28 May 1918.

18GW685, 18GW681, 18GW674. French soldiers with flamethrowers cleared the cellars of Germans in Cantigny, 28 May 1918. American infantry carried on their advance a further half kilometre.

18GW666 American Vickers machine gun team in a position to lay down fire on any counter-attack and provide covering fire for their fellow infantrymen.

18GW688 US soldiers killed in the fighting have been gathered for burial once the battle is over.

18GW686 An American officer looks on as French soldiers search German prisoners taken during the fighting at Cantigny.

18GW687 One of the many German dead awaiting collection and burial at Cantigny.

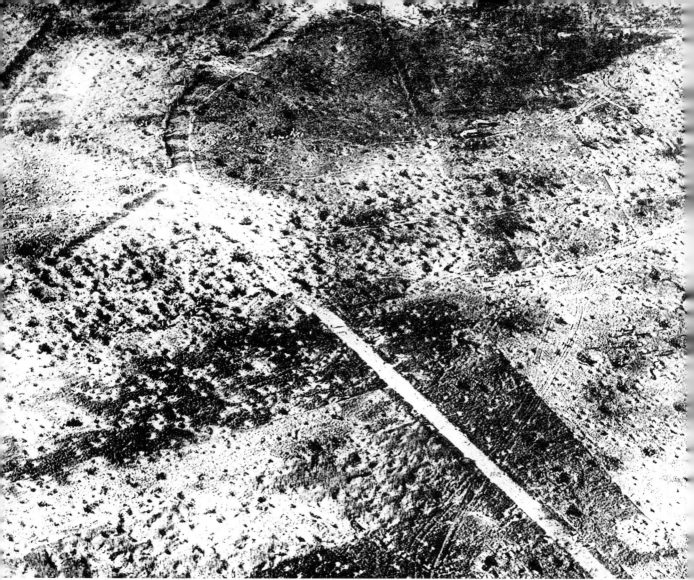

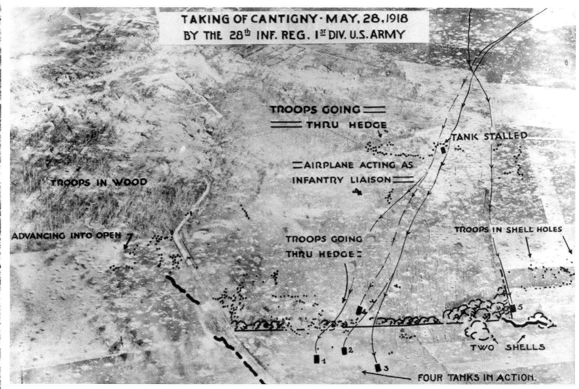

TAKING OF CANTIGNY · MAY, 28, 1918
BY THE 28th INF. REG. 1st DIV. U.S. ARMY

TROOPS GOING THRU HEDGE

TANK STALLED

AIRPLANE ACTING AS INFANTRY LIAISON

TROOPS IN WOOD

TROOPS IN SHELL HOLES

ADVANCING INTO OPEN

TROOPS GOING THRU HEDGE

TWO SHELLS

FOUR TANKS IN ACTION.

18GW689, 18GW683. Photograph of the battlefield at Cantigny taken during the action and annotated photograph showing the direction of the advance past the village: soldiers shown as dots and the direction and progress of the six supporting French crewed tanks.

Captain C.R. Hueber, second in command of the Second Battalion 28th Infantry Regiment, during the attack on Cantigny, 28 May 1918, gives the following account:

Lieutenant Colonel Robert Jayne Maxey commanded the Second Battalion, 28th Infantry Regiment, in the attack upon Cantigny. In the early part of the engagement he was advancing with the first line of the Infantry when he was wounded in the neck by a shell fragment which later caused his death. He was placed upon a litter and was being carried to the first aid station when he insisted upon being taken to my position as he said he had some orders that he wanted to turn over to me. Upon reaching the position of my company, he ordered the litter bearers to lay him down and go and get me. I was about 200 yards away, superintending the construction of a strongpoint. When I reached the colonel I found him upon the litter and helpless, but he could speak and gave me full and complete instructions as to how to carry on. He had me get his map and showed me on the map where the positions were to be and how to defend them. All this time we were under heavy machine-gun fire with an occasional artillery shot. He showed utter disregard for his own wound and thought of nothing but the success of the operation nor would he proceed on his way until he was sure that I understood everything, thereby inspiring great devotion and courage.

18GW692 Dressing Station in the fields at Cantigny where the enemy wounded received the same attention as the American wounded.

18GW690 Lieutenant Colonel Robert Jayne Maxey commanded the Second Battalion, 28th Infantry Regiment, 1st Division, AEF. He died of wounds the day of the attack.

18GW695 Ambulances roll into Paris and American Military Hospital One.

18GW691 A Cantigny first aid post in a sunken road. In the original caption we are told:
It was all in a day's work so Private Barnes, wounded at Cantigny, takes it philosophically.

18GW693 A wounded German at Cantigny Dressing Station is being lifted onto a stretcher and carried to a waiting ambulance.

18GW696 Wounded Doughboys enjoying a joke as they arrive at Military Hospital One, Paris.

18GW694 Prisoners captured at Cantigny marching through Le Mesnil St Firmin, 28 May 1918.

18GW705 As men of the US 1st Division were driving the Germans back at Cantigny their comrades in the 32nd Infantry Division were marching onto German sovereign territory at Sentheim, Alsace, 29 May 1918. The men turning off the road are Company A, 125th Infantry Regiment, among the first Americans to set foot on Germany.

18GW699 Brigadier General Fox Conner, Chief of Operations to General Pershing, recognized the gravity of the German threat to Paris and ordered elements of the US 3rd Infantry Division to block their advance.

18GW699 General Joseph T. Dickman, commanding the 3rd Infantry Division.

ON THE RIVER MARNE AT CHÂTEAU-THIERRY and BELLEAU WOOD in June 1918 the American Expeditionary Force played a key role in halting the German army's thrust towards Paris, during what became known as the Second Battle of the Marne. On 1 June, when it seemed that the enemy would capture the French capital, the American 2nd Division was rushed to Château-Thierry to block the German advance. In July an Allied counter offensive pivoting on Château-Thierry was launched and the Americans attacked across the Marne. The Allied aim was to reduce and obliterate the enemy occupied bulge into their territory which threatened Paris.

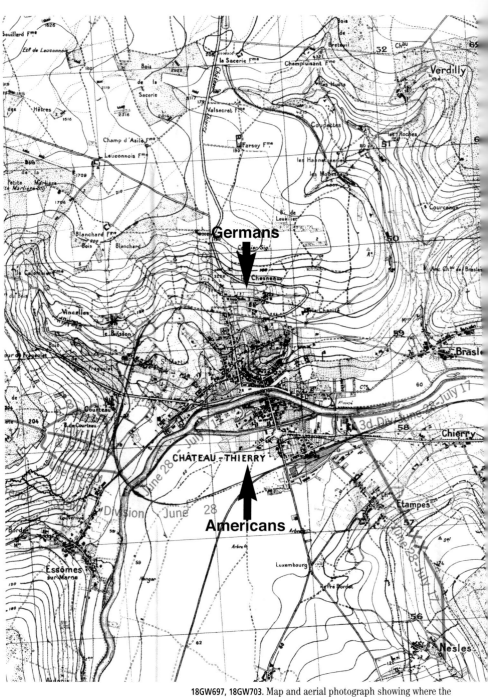

18GW697, 18GW703. Map and aerial photograph showing where the Americans stopped the German thrust towards Paris.

18GW704 Men of the 3rd Infantry Division boarding lorries to take them to the Marne river crossings at Château-Thierry.

18GW701 American artillery transports arriving in Château-Thierry, June 1918.

18GW706 The Germans were stopped when they reached this point, the destroyed bridge over the Marne, at Château-Thierry.

18GW667 American machine gunners of Company A, 7th Machine Gun Battalion, at Château-Thierry, June 1918 The weapon is the Hotchkiss Mle 1914 which became the French infantry standard in 1917. The American Expeditionary Forces purchased 7,000 Mle 1914 Hotchkiss machine guns and used them extensively in the fighting in 1918.

18GW707 Some of the men who stopped the Germans: soldiers of the 9th Machine Gun Battalion, 3rd Infantry Division. Seventeen machine gun positions were set up in time to bring the enemy advance to a halt.

18GW711 French and American troops surveying the damage in Château-Thierry after the fighting.

18GW710, 18GW708. German dead awaiting burial by the French and Americans outside Château-Thierry after the fighting.

18GW708 American artillery on the north bank of the Marne moving through Château-Thierry on a street leading from one of the broken bridges after the Germans had been pushed back.

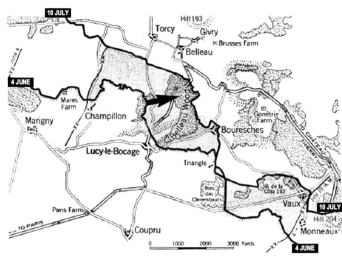

Operations of the 2nd Infantry Division 4 June to 10 July 1918. The American 5th and 6th Marine Regiments were ordered to capture Belleau Wood and clear it of Germans. They cleared Belleau Wood of the German Army by 26 June, at the cost of almost 2,000 Marines dead and 8,000 injured. The battle proved to be the end of the last major German offensive of the war.

18GW714 Major General Omar Bundy commanded 2nd Infantry Division and the operations against German positions in Belleau Wood.

18GW717 Officers of 2nd Battalion, 6th Marine Regiment (6th Marines) during the fighting at Belleau Wood, June 18, 1918.

18GW715 Gunnery Sergeant Ernest August Janson (alias Charles Hoffman) served with the 49th Company, 5th Regiment, in its actions at Belleau Wood.

On June 6, 1918 Gunnery Sergeant Janson was awarded both the Army and Navy Medals of Honor. Citation: *For conspicuous gallantry and intrepidity above and beyond the call of duty in action with the enemy near Château-Thierry, France, 6 June, 1918. Immediately after the company to which G/Sgt. Janson belonged had reached its objective on Hill 142, several hostile counterattacks were launched against the line before the new position had been consolidated. G/Sgt. Janson was attempting to organize a position on the north slope of the hill when he saw twelve of the enemy, armed with five light machine guns, crawling toward his group. Giving the alarm, he rushed the hostile detachment, bayoneted the two leaders and forced the others to flee, abandoning their guns. His quick action, initiative and courage drove the enemy from a position from which they could have swept the hill with machine gun fire and forced the withdrawal of our troops.* The French Médaille militaire, the Montenegrin Silver Medal, the Portuguese Cruz de Guerra, and the Italian Croce di Guerra were also awarded to him for the same act.

18GW718 Members of the 77th Company, 6th Machine Gun Battalion, and French poilus near Belleau. Note the burly French soldier seeming to be clasping the hand of the Doughboy – perhaps demonstating for the camera the close comaraderie enjoyed by the Allied soldiers fighting the Boche invaders.

18GW713 The village of Vaux as elements of the 9th and 23rd Infantry Regiments of the 2nd Division entered the the streets, 1 July 1918. The town had been subjected to heavy shelling by the Americans and dead Germans litter the streets. Targets for the guns had been pinpointed by a French stonemason who had previously lived in the village.

18GW731 John Joseph 'Black Jack' Pershing, commander of the American Expeditionary Force, wrote in his summary of the fighting by the US 2nd Infantry Division:

> *The enemy having been halted, the Second Division commenced a series of vigorous attacks on 4 June, which resulted in the capture of Belleau Wood after very severe fighting. The village of Bouresches was taken soon after and on 1 July Vaux was captured. In these operations the Second Division met with most desperate resistance by Germany's best troops.*

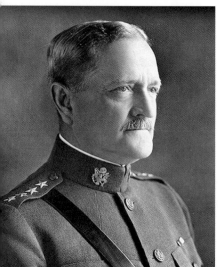

18GW730 The battlefield at Belleau Wood after it had been captured by the United States Marine Corps.

> *The Fourth Marine Brigade captured Hill 142 and the village of Bouresches on 6 June, 1918 and, in the words of General Pershing, sturdily held its ground against the enemy's best divisions and completely cleared Bois de Belleau of the enemy on 26 June, 1918.*

18GW732 The village of Vaux captured from the enemy and after it was occupied by the 9th and 23rd Infantry Regiments, 2nd Infantry Division.

18GW728 A photograph taken by an aircraft of the US Air Service showing the German bombardment of Bouresches Wood. Bouresches village was captured late in the evening of 6 June 1918, by Lieutenant James F Robertson, United States Marine Corps, along with twenty men of his platoon.

18GW719 Three crew of a 37 mm gun (called the 'pound wonder', according to the original caption), in the front line at Diefmatten, Alsace, 25 June 1918: Sergeant Charles Quick, Corporal Mark Young and Private Albert Lull of the 126th Infantry Regiment.

18GW720 Men of Company K, 127th Infantry Regiment, 32nd Division manning a trench block at Benholz, Alsace, 1 July 1918.

18GW722 From a breach in a wall French Poilus and a Yank observe the effect of enemy artillery fire.

18GW721 Private Leo R Hahn, sniper, Intelligence Section, 127th Infantry Regiment, 32nd Division, in trenches at Benholtz, Alsace, 1 July 1918.

18GW724 A wounded soldier being brought in to the American Field Hospital near Montreuil, 7 June 1918.

18GW725 Poison gas victim (marked on the forehead with a 'T') being carried out to a waiting ambulance, Montreuil.

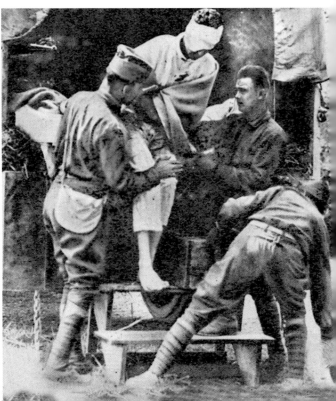

18GW723 Major General William G Haan, commander of the 32nd Infantry Division, leaves his headquarters at Massevaux to review troops, accompanied by French officers. The 32nd Division (Wisconsin and Michigan) was earning a reputation for fierce fighting and were being referred to as *Les Terribles*.

18GW726 Lightly wounded arriving at the Field Hospital, Montreuil, 7 June 1918.

18GW727 A specially converted carriage of a hospital train full of wounded being transported to a base hospital.

18GW733 American graves on the edge of the village of Vaux.

18GW729 Marine Corps men wearing French gas masks.

18GW735 Battle experienced non commissioned officers leave for the States to help train the US Army; here seen off by the local children.

18GW737 Brigadier General Charles T. Menoher, commanding the 42nd Infantry Division (Rainbow Division) in the Champagne-Marne offensive and in the successful Allied offensives of Saint Mihiel and Meuse-Argonne. Menoher was succeeded by General Douglas MacArthur almost at the end of the war.

18GW738 General Douglas MacArthur, St Juvin, Ardeness, France, 3 November 1918.

18GW736 Fast becoming hardened veterans, these men of Company B, 166th Infantry Regiment (4th Ohio) 42nd Division (Rainbow Division) are entering La Ferté-sous-Jouarre, 23 July, 1918. Two days later the Rainbow Division relieved the 26th Infantry Division and extended its front, relieving a French Division.

18GW739, 18GW740. Soldiers of the 111th Infantry Regiment, 28th Infantry Division, resting at Château-Thierry while on their way to take part in the counter offensive to drive the Germans back from the salient threatening Paris, 21 July, 1918.

18GW742 Château-Thierry where the Americans crossed the Marne, July 1918.

18GW743 The drive is on to push the Germans out of the Marne salient. Wagons of the 150th Field Artillery (1st Indiana Field Artillery) passing through Château-Thierry, July 1918.

18GW741 Major General Charles Henry Muir, commanding 28th Infantry Division.

18GW744 Reserves of the 1st Infantry Division waiting for the order to move up to the line at Coeuvres-et-Valsery, 17 July 1918, to relieve a brigade of French Moroccans. The following day they were thrown in to an attack on Berzy-le-Sec and the heights above Soissons. After four days of constant fighting the Division advanced seven miles, taking 3,500 prisoners and captured 68 field guns. They appear to resent the presence of the Signal Corps photographer.

18GW748 Going over the top, Americans of the 1st Infantry Division, commanded by General Charles Summerall, carried out the Big Red One's first major attack during the bloody three-day drive near Soissons in late July 1918. Along with the rest of the Corps, it relentlessly attacked until a key German rail line was severed, forcing a major withdrawal of the enemy's forces.

18GW750 General Charles P. Summerall.

18GW747 Coming to close quarters with the enemy: these men of the 166th Infantry Regiment check shell damaged farm buildings at Villers sur Fère for enemy snipers, 30 July 1918.

18GW749 A sunken road littered with dead Germans and their equipment, killed during desperate fighting with the 16th Infantry Regiment, 1st Division, in its attack on Missy-au-Bois, late July 1918.

18GW752 A field littered with the American dead belonging to the 167th Infantry Regiment who fell during the advance toward Fère-en-Tardenois. The Americans were employing the tactics of attack abandoned by the French and the British – advancing in extended line in a similar manner used during the American Civil War. They would begin to learn but not until they had suffered heavy casualties.

18GW751 Dawn attack, 04.30 hrs, 18 July 1918. Men of the 103rd Infantry Regiment, 26th Division, can be seen advancing at the edge of the wood. The field in front of them is being swept by machine-gun fire and bursting shells. They reached their objective, the village of Torcy, in thirty-five minutes.

18GW745 Soldiers from the 166th Infantry Regiment, 42nd Infantry (the Rainbow Division) receive a heartfelt welcome from the M. and Mme Baloux as they liberate a French village in 1918. Their deliverers are Philip Tangor and Allen Floyd. Note the French *Fusil Mitrailleur* light machine gun over Tangor's shoulder.

18GW755, 18GW756. Men of the 2nd Battalion, 126th Infantry Regiment (Michigan National Guard) assembling for an attack near Coutmont, 1 August 1918.

18GW757 German dead at Mezy, 21 July 1918.

The only American to receive the nation's four highest awards:

Medal of Honor
Distinguished Service Cross
Distinguished Service Medal
National Security Medal

18GW753 Major William Joseph 'Wild Bill' Donovan, commanded the 1st Battalion, 165th Regiment, 42nd Division.

After carrying out a rescue under fire, he was awarded the Croix de Guerre. He also won the Distinguished Service Cross for leading an assault during the Aisne-Marne campaign, in which hundreds of members of his regiment died. Donovan's remarkable level of endurance, which far exceeded that of the much younger soldiers under his command, led those men to give him the nickname 'Wild Bill', which stuck with him for the rest of his life. Appointed chief of staff of the 165th Regiment, Donovan fought in a further battle that took place near Landres-et-Saint-Georges on 14-15 October, 1918. He was wounded in the knee but refused to be evacuated and continued to direct his men until even American tanks were turning back under withering German fire. Donovan was awarded an Oak Leaf Cluster.

In the Second World War he was the head of the OSS, the forerunner of the CIA.

18GW758 Dead of the 167th Infantry Regiment (Alabama) after the advance on Fere-en-Tardenois. Rifle is indicator to the gravediggers.

18GW762 Americans of the 38th Infantry Regiment killed in hand to hand fighting at Merzy.

18GW761 The body of a doughboy hung on the wire.

18GW760 American gravediggers burying the dead in the final weeks of the war.

18GW759 Germans killed in a bayonet charge by men of the 125th Infantry Regiment at Cierges.

18GW763 An important part of modern warfare – the collecting, identifying and removal from the battlefield of those killed.

18GW764 A Prussian Guard trench and machine gun post, the occupants having been bayonetted by Americans of the 42nd Inafntry Division as they advanced.

18GW765 A priority target for the American infantryman: these two German soldiers were operating a Flammenwerfer – flamethrower – attempting to burn out the men occupying these farm buildings; blackened farm equipment gives evidence of the fierce flames that wrecked them. Carried by specially trained assault teams, German flamethrowers were highly effective weapons that would either drive men from their defensive positions or simply incinerate them.

18GW731 A burial party of the 42nd Infantry Division, these groups were kept busy for days digging graves for the dead that littered the fields and woods following the advance beyond Château-Thierry. Beuvardes, France, 30 July 1918.

18GW773 Despite the wholesale slaughter being engaged in on a massive scale on the Western Front, regular appeals for the Almighty's favour was carried on by armies of both sides. Here members of the 101st Field Signal Battalion (formerly 1st Massachusetts Field Signal Battalion) have sought out 'holy ground' among the ruins of a church destroyed by shell fire for an outdoor church service near the blood-soaked ground of Verdun, France. They are singing a hymn, which doubtless praises the Prince of Peace, 18 October 1918.

18GW771 American gunners in France operating a BL 8 inch Howitzer Mk VI,They were designed by Vickers in Britain and produced by all four British artillery manufacturers, but mainly by Armstrong and one American company. They were the equivalents of the German 21 cm Morser 16 and in British service were used similarly to the BL 9.2-inch howitzer, but were quicker to manufacture and more mobile. They delivered a 200 lb shell to a distance of 12,300 yards. They had limited service in the British Army in the Second World War before being converted to the new 7.2-inch calibre. They also equipped a small number of Australian and Canadian batteries in the Great War.

18GW769 An example of the deep, fortified trenches affording shelter from shelling that faced the 32nd Infantry Division along the Kriemhilde Stellung.

18GW774 American troops in action with a 75 mm French field gun. It was the first field gun to include a hydro-pneumatic recoil mechanism, which kept the gun's trail and wheels perfectly still during the firing sequence, hence, it could deliver fifteen rounds per minute on its target and with an experienced crew as many as thirty rounds per minute. The American Expeditionary Force was supplied with upwards of 2,000 of these weapons.

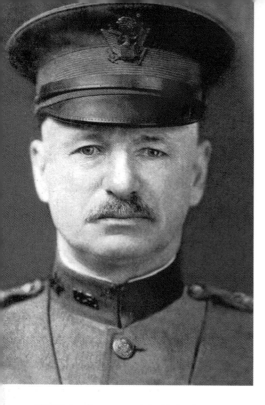

18GW770 William George Haan, commanding the 32nd Infantry Division.

18GW766 American troops of the 32nd Infantry Division on German soil at Massevaux, Alsace, reviewed by their commander Major General William G. Haan, accompanied by General Boisson, French commander in that sector.

18GW779 An American despatch rider on a Harley-Davidson; when the United States entered the war in April 1917 the company upped production, delivering over 20,000 motorcycles to support the military.

18GW767 The band of the 166th Regiment (Columbus, Ohio), 42nd Infantry Division.

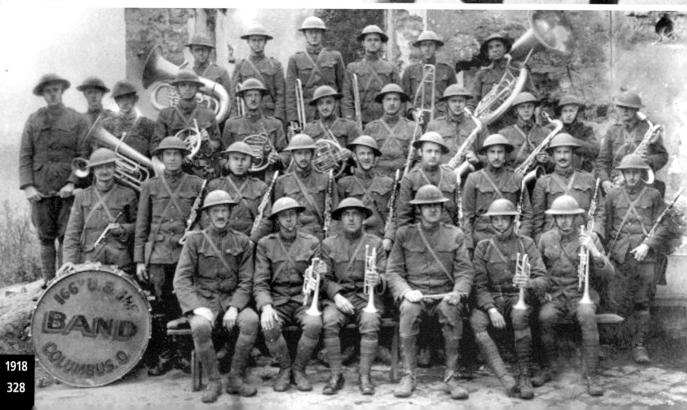

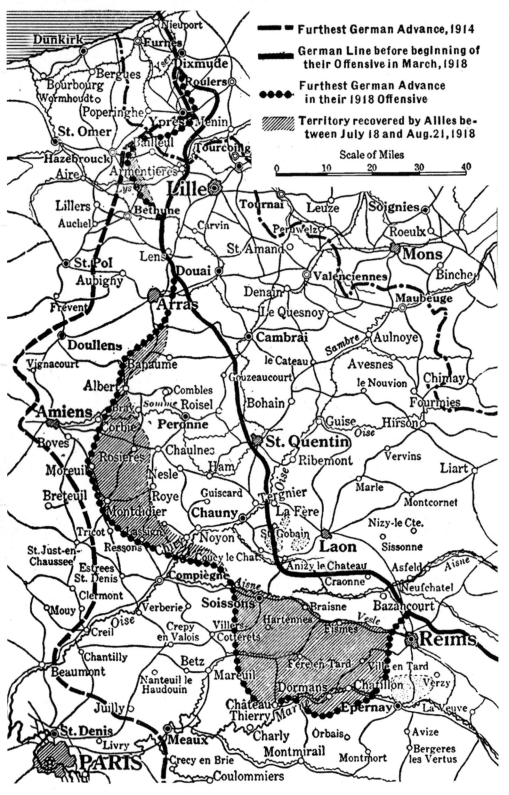

Furthest German Advance, 1914

German Line before beginning of their Offensive in March, 1918

Furthest German Advance in their 1918 Offensive

Territory recovered by Allies between July 18 and Aug.21,1918

Scale of Miles

0   10   20   30   40

The shaded areas indicate how close the Germans came to their planned breakthrough, utilising the divisions released from the Eastern Front in the Spring of 1918. The Allies fell back but held and with the Americans fully playing their part, the Germans were driven back and the bulges straightened. It was now time for the French, British and Americans to go over to the offensive.

18GW778 A German machine gun crew, an officer and five men, strike up varying poses for the camera. The Kaiser's Spring Offensive had made great territory gains and Paris had been threatened, but the line had held and the breakthrough and collapse of the Allies had not happened. The American Expeditionary Force was beginning to make a difference as Pershing's army began to learn the art of waging a modern war.

18GW775 An American soldier lies dead before a captured German machine gun nest. There are three weapon apertures, each with two compartments to house a machine gun, making a total of six weapons able to bring down a great weight of fire power to command direct approaches.

1918

332

18GW780, 18GW781. Fierce hand to hand fighting took place on this important communication road used by the Germans to distribute men and supplies throughout the newly captured territory. The road's loss made the Château-Thierry salient untenable and the demoralized Germans began to pull back.

18GW776, 18GW782. Near Château-Thierry two Yanks stand behind the corpses of some recently killed Germans. German casualties were began to mount. The second week in August saw an all out Allied attack along the Western Front.

18GW786 Men of Company K 128th Infantry Regiment, 32nd Division, in position at Valpries farm before the town of Juvigny, 29 August 1918. They are are just 300 yards from the crest, which is mid way between them and the Germans. Juvigny was captured the next day. French General Mangin praised his allies:

...for the brilliant conduct and splendid courage displayed in taking the town, the memory of which will remain for us and will place in history the glorious deeds of the 32nd Division and its able and valiant General Haan.

18GW783 Headquarters of the 58th Infantry Regiment at Chéry-Chartreuve Farm, 9 August 1918. Left to right: Lieutenant J A Burton, 8th Field Signal Battalion; Second Lieutenant G. L. Morrow, Signal Officer; Colonel C F Armistead, commanding the 58th; Captain John Meurisse, French liaison officer; Sergeant Major G I Schrenck; and Major T M Baird, surgeon.

18GW785 French Renault FT-17 tanks moving through American infantry of the 32nd Division to support French units operating on the American left flank.

18GW784 A former German machine gun nest on a house top in the village of St Gilles is now occupied by Americans and their machine gun.

18GW787 Lieutenant Colonel George S Patton commanding the American 1st Tank Battalion, with a French Renault tank, Summer 1918. On 10 November, 1917 Patton had been assigned to establish the AEF Light Tank School. He was promoted to major in January 1918. He received the first ten tanks on March 23, 1918 at the Tank School at Bourg. He was promoted to lieutenant colonel 3 April, 1918. In August 1918, he was placed in charge of the US 1st Provisional Tank Brigade. He commanded an American-crewed Renault FT tanks at the Battle of Saint-Mihiel and was wounded during the Meuse-Argonne Offensive in September. Patton wrote in a letter to his wife: *The bullet went into the front of my left leg and came out just at the crack of my bottom about two inches to the left of my rectum. It was fired at about fifty yards so made a hole about the size of a dollar where it came out.* He returned to duty at the end of October but saw no further action before the end of the war. For his actions, Patton received the Distinguished Service Cross. For his leadership of the brigade and tank school, he was awarded the Distinguished Service Medal.

On 24 July the Allies held a conference and agreed that all their forces should go on the offensive; their joint course of action was as follows:
(a) Continuation of the reduction of the Marne salient to secure as a minimum result the release of the Paris-Chalons railway line.
(b) Reduction of the Amiens salient, thus securing the release of the Paris-Amien railway line.
(c) Reduction of the St Mihiel salient.
(d) Liberation of the coal mining regions in the north and driving of the enemy away from the ports of Dunkerque and Calais.

Reduction of the St Mihiel salient was made the task of Pershing's American army. From the German point of view, occupation of the salient covered their strategic supply centre at Metz and the Briey iron ore and steel production basin. It would be the first large scale operation by an American army.

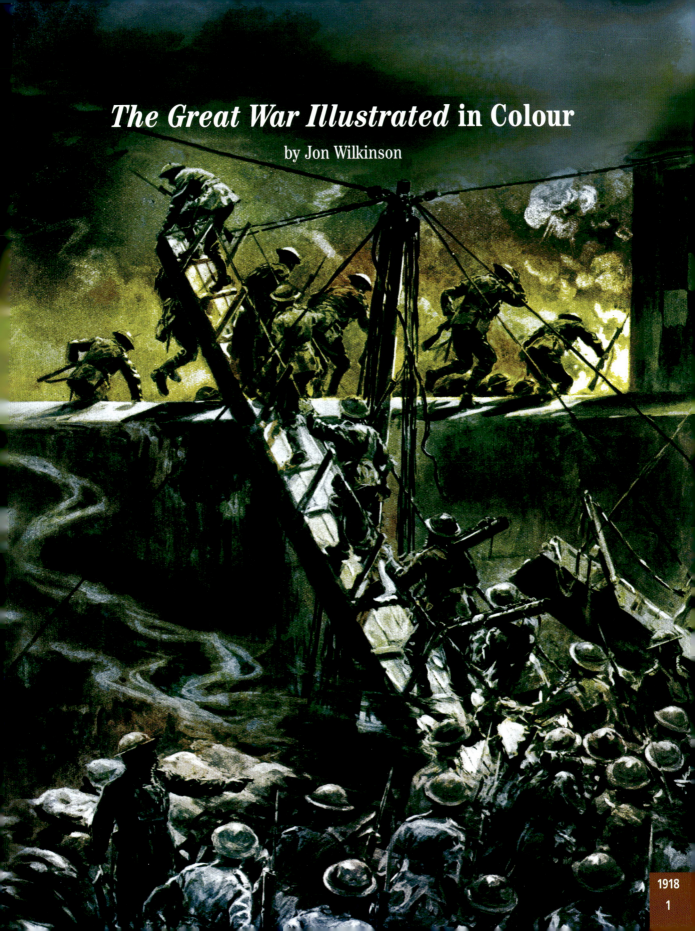

The Great War Illustrated in Colour

by Jon Wilkinson

18GWco02 Concrete submarine pens ensured protection against attack from the air. The port of Zeebrugge, with the neighboring port of Ostend, became a thorn in the side of the British, French and Belgians by reason of their use as bases for destroyers and submarines. Canals connected the inland town of Bruges with Zeebrugge and Ostend and U-boats, destroyers and torpedo boats sailed from their pens at Brugge to the open sea to prey on the busy shipping lanes. Zeebrugge was especially useful, protected as it was from the rough sea by a crescent-shaped mole thirty feet high enclosing the harbour.

18co05 A British naval raiding party, under Vice Admiral Sir Roger Keyes, undertook to damage the stone mole at Zeebrugge seriously and to block the entrances to the canals both at Zeebrugge and at Ostend by sinking the hulks of old ships in the channels. The main assault ship chosen was the armoured cruiser HMS *Vindictive*. She was fitted out with supporting armament for the raid. The total number of personnel required for various aspects of the raid, including the block ships, amounted to 86 officers and 1,698 men *Vindictive* was only able to carry the First Wave of the assaulting force. Two shallow draught Mersey ferries carried the rest.

18co03, 18co04. German marine infantry manning positions on the Belgian coast and German gunners guarding the Mole. Raids by the allies were expected.

18co06. The Mersey ferryboats *Iris* right and *Daffodil* in the centre.

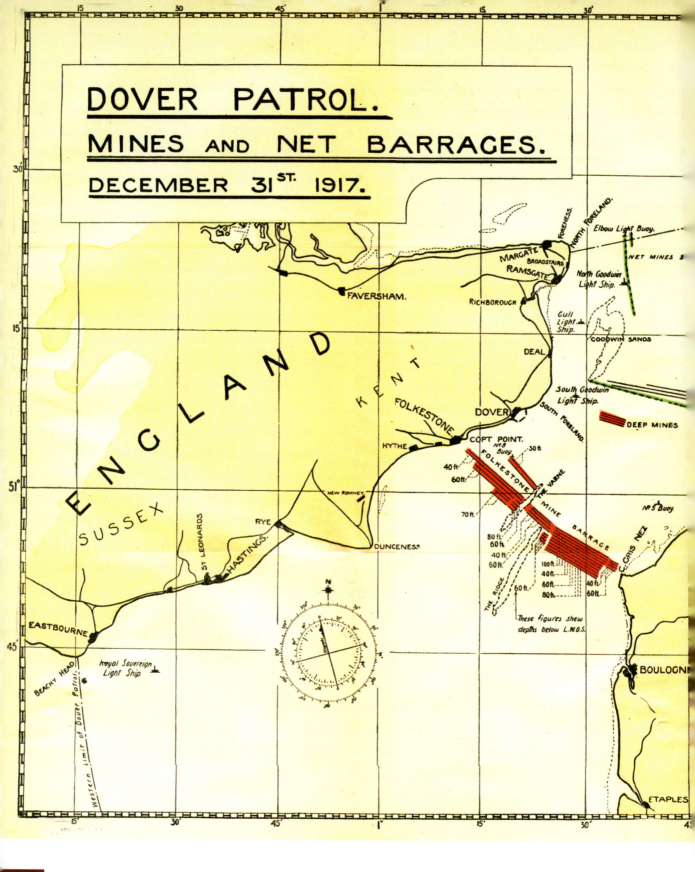

DOVER PATROL.
MINES AND NET BARRAGES.
DECEMBER 31ST. 1917.

ENGLAND

KENT

SUSSEX

FAVERSHAM.

MARGATE
RAMSGATE
BROADSTAIRS
FORENESS.
NORTH FORELAND.
Elbow Light Buoy.
NET MINES B
North Goodwin Light Ship.
Gull Light Ship.
GOODWIN SANDS
RICHBOROUGH
DEAL
South Goodwin Light Ship.
DOVER
SOUTH FORELAND.

DEEP MINES

FOLKESTONE
HYTHE
COPT POINT.
No 8 Buoy
30 ft.
40 ft.
60 ft.
FOLKESTONE
THE VARNE
MINE BARRAGE
No 5 Buoy.
C. GRIS NEZ.
70 ft.
80 ft.
60 ft.
40 ft.
60 ft.
100 ft.
40 ft.
60 ft.
80 ft.
40 ft.
60 ft.
THE RIDGE
60 ft.
These figures shew depths below L.W.O.S.

NEW ROMNEY
DUNGENESS

RYE
ST LEONARDS
HASTINGS.

EASTBOURNE
BEACHY HEAD.
Royal Sovereign Light Ship
Western limit of Dover Patrol.

N

BOULOGNE

ETAPLES

1917
4

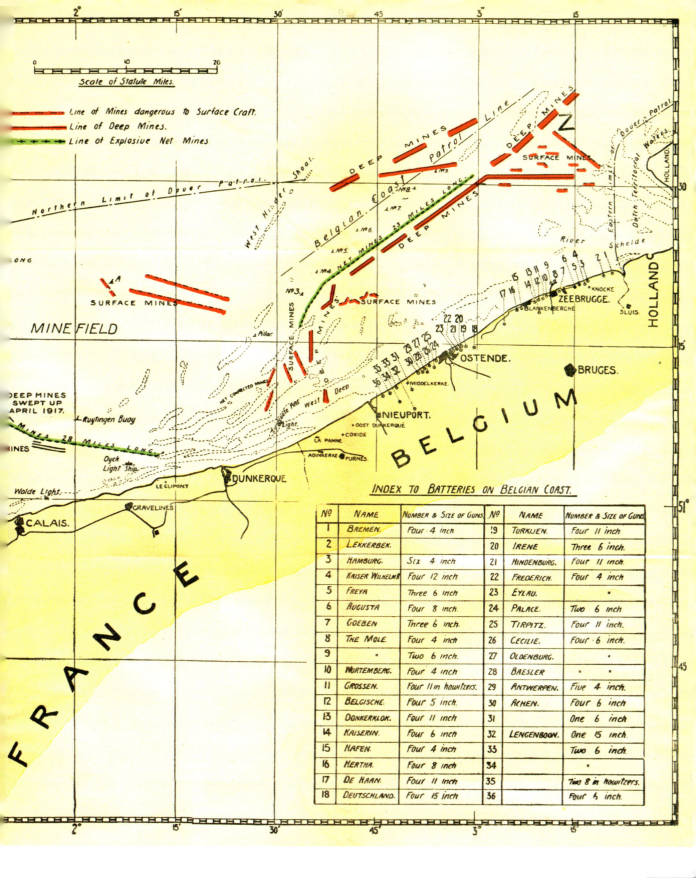

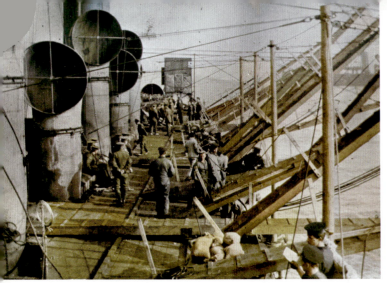

18Gco08 Deck of the *Vindictive* with specially constructed gangplanks that could be lowered to connect with the Mole to discharge the raiding party.

18co10 Royal Marines demonstrating their fighting garb. They were issued with khaki for the raid.

18co13 An artist's impression of Royal Marines storming up the specially constructed gang planks bridging the gap between between the deck of the *Vindictive* and the Mole wall.

18co09 An artist's impression of the *Vindictive* against the Mole wall.

18co15 HMS *Vindictive* sailed into Dover at 8 am on the morning of 23 April 1918. Crowds cheered her arrival back from the raid,

18co11 British submarine of the same class as HMS *C3* which rammed the mole packed with explosives, under the command of Lieutenant Richard Sandford. An artist's impression of the incident.

18co14 After the battle: British dead on the Mole parapet.

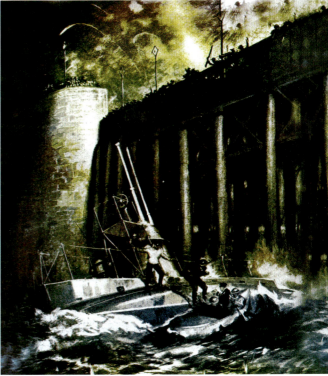

18co16 The substantial breach in the Mole viaduct caused by 10,000 kilos of high explosive delivered with accuracy by the crew of HMS *C3* under the command of Lieutenant Richard Sandford.

18co17 A post raid aerial view taken at high tide looking north, with the block ships in place.

18co18 Smoke coming from the prow of the block ship *Intrepid*.

18co19 Ship movement was seriously impeded by the placing of the three blockships, HMS *Intrepid*, HMS *Iphigenia* and HMS *Thetis*.

18co21, 18co24. When HMS *Vindictive* sailed into Dover after the raid cheering crowds fell silent – her superstructure was riddled with bullet holes and by huge rents from shrapnel shards. The fighting foretop on *Vindictive*, where Sergeant Finch earned a VC. During the action two heavy shells made direct hits on the foretop, which was completely exposed to enemy concentration of fire. All in the top were killed or disabled except Sergeant Finch, who was, however, severely wounded; nevertheless, he remained in the battered, exposed position. He once more got a Lewis gun into action, and kept up a continuous fire, harassing the enemy on the Mole.

18co20 The *Vindictive* against a pier at Ostend and clearly not blocking the channel.

18co22, 18co23. The Stokes mortar position situated beneath the flamethrower hut on HMS *Vindictive*. A massive clean-up operation was carried out by the crew and marines.

German Enperor
Kaiser William II

Generalfeldmarshall
Paul von Hindenburg

General der Infantrie
Erich von Luddendorff

18co29, 18co30 Storm troops leading the attack on the Allied positions. The collapse of the Russian Army in 1917 allowed the Germans to concentrate substantial extra forces on the Western Front. Ludendorff prepared a massive attack which was launched in Spring 1918, before the American Expeditionary Forces were sufficiently reinforced to present a real danger.

1918

11

18co31 A 17cm *mittlerer Minenwerfer* Medium Trench Mortar crew in action.

18co32 British soldiers killed in the fighting with the advancing German *Sturmtruppen* March, April 1918.

18co33, 18co34. German shock troops advancing, after breaking through barbed wire. These would likely be training photographs.

18co35 German shock troops sheltering behind a wrecked French Schneider CA-1 tank.

18co36 German *Sturmtruppen* photographed at the time of their attack – most probably a training photograph as the cameraman appears to have been standing upright and therefore in the line of fire.

The massive German Spring Offensive – the *Kaiserschlacht* had ground to a halt. All-out victory and a breakthrough to the Channel coast was not achieved and the German armies were exhausted and in exposed positions. The morale of the German soldier suffered a blow when he saw the amount and quality of the Allied food supplies. The territorial gain resulted in a number of salients, which greatly increased the length of the line that would have to be defended when Allied reinforcements gave the Allies the initiative. By July 1918, the German superiority of numbers on the Western Front had sunk to 207 divisions to 203 Allied, a negligible lead, which was being reversed weekly as more American troops arrived. German manpower was exhausted. They had lost many of their best-trained men as the stormtrooper tactics had them leading the attacks. General Ludendorff abandoned all hope of obtaining a decisive decision on the Western Front before the Americans appeared on the battlefields in strength.

18co37 An élite German warrior, a member of the *Sturmtruppen*. He had tried and failed; now it was the turn of the Allies to gather strength for the massive counter attack that would bring the madness to an end.

18co38 British soldiers in Péronne in August at the beginning of the Advance to Victory.

18co41 The southern bank of the River Aisne, 27 May 1918. Soldiers of the Royal Worcestershire Regiment take up positions to repel advancing Germans.

18co43 A British Lewis gun team ready for action in a sunken road.

18co42 German machine gunners were extremely effective in their deadly work and were regarded with considerable respect by Allied infantry. Silencing these gun crews was imperative in every assault. The weapon is a Maxim 08/15, capable of firing 600 rounds per minute.

18GWco44 The British Gun Carrier Mk I, The gun was a 60-pounder (or 6-inch howitzer). This one is photographed near the village of Irles in the last week of August 1918.

1918
22

18co45 Attack on the Hindenburg Line, 29 September 1918.

18co46 Attack on the Hindenburg Line, British Mk V tanks carrying 'cribs' to help crossing the trenches, and troops going forward near Bellicourt 29 September 1918. Note the German prisoners mingled with the Tommies.

18co47 A British battery of 18-pounder field guns in action on the old Somme battlefield in October 1918.

18co48 There were others who would pay the supreme sacrifice to the god of war: The National Shell Filling Factory, Chilwell, filled high explosives into some nine million shells since it began production in January 1916. On 1 July 1918 much of the factory was destroyed in an explosion of eight tons of TNT. A total of 134 people were killed, of whom only thirty-two could be identified; and a further 250 were injured.

Minister of Munitions Winston Churchill sent the following telegram:
Please accept my sincere sympathy with you all in the misfortune that has overtaken your fine Factory and in the loss of valuable lives. Those who have perished have died at their stations on the field of duty and those who have lost their dear ones should fortify themselves with this thought, the courage and spirit shown by all concerned, both men and women, command our admiration, and the decision to which you have all come to carry on without a break is worthy of the spirit which animates our soldiers in the field. I trust the injured are receiving every care.

The war is almost over and another winter in the trenches will not have to be endured – 'We'll drink to that!'

PRE-WAR AFRICA

——	INTERNATIONAL BOUNDARIES
······	TERRITORIAL BOUNDARIES
▬	BRITISH
▬	FRENCH
▬	BELGIAN
▬	PORTUGUESE
▬	ITALIAN
▬	SPANISH
▬	GERMAN

TOGOLAND. At the outbreak of the Great War in 1914, the German colony of Togoland was drawn into the conflict. It was invaded and quickly overrun by British and French forces during the Togoland Campaign and placed under military rule.

CAMEROON. the British invaded Cameroon from Nigeria in 1914 in the Kamerun campaign, with the last German fort in the country surrendering in February 1916

SOUTH WEST AFRICA. In 1915, German South West Africa was invaded by the Western Allies in the form of South African and British forces. After the war its administration was taken over by the Union of South Africa (a Dominion of the British Empire) and the territory was administered as South West Africa under a League of Nations mandate.

GERMAN EAST AFRICA. The commander of German forces, Paul von Lettow-Vorbeck, for four years held in check a much larger force of 300,000 British, Belgian and Portuguese troops with a force of 14,000 men (3,000 Germans and 11,000 Africans). He was the only German commander successfully to invade British territory during the Great War. His exploits in the campaign have been described 'as the greatest single guerrilla operation in history, and the most successful'.

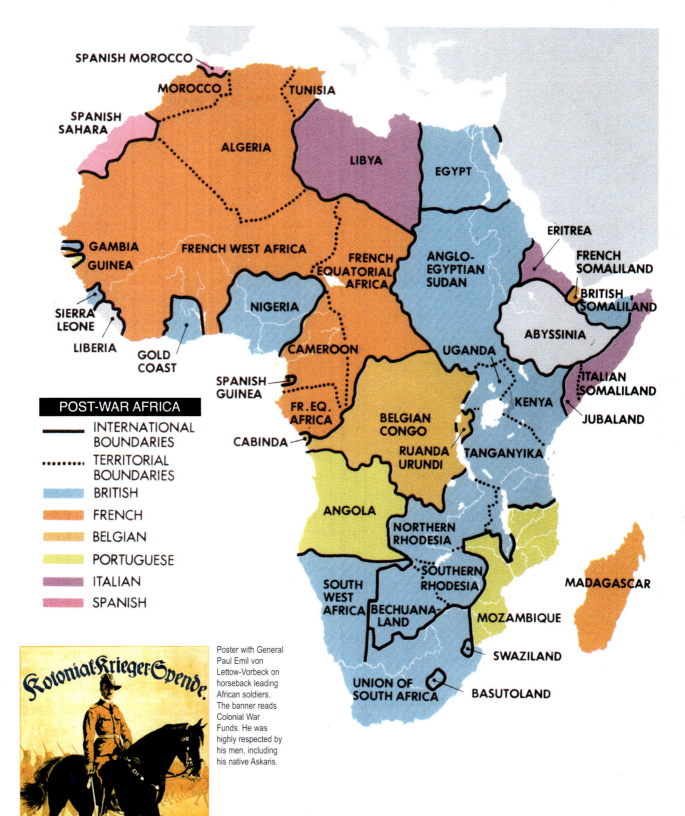

POST-WAR AFRICA

INTERNATIONAL
BOUNDARIES
······ TERRITORIAL
BOUNDARIES
BRITISH
FRENCH
BELGIAN
PORTUGUESE
ITALIAN
SPANISH

SPANISH MOROCCO
MOROCCO
TUNISIA
SPANISH
SAHARA
ALGERIA
LIBYA
EGYPT
ERITREA
GAMBIA
GUINEA
FRENCH WEST AFRICA
FRENCH
EQUATORIAL
AFRICA
ANGLO-
EGYPTIAN
SUDAN
FRENCH
SOMALILAND
BRITISH
SOMALILAND
SIERRA
LEONE
LIBERIA
GOLD
COAST
NIGERIA
CAMEROON
UGANDA
ABYSSINIA
ITALIAN
SOMALILAND
SPANISH
GUINEA
FR. EQ.
AFRICA
KENYA
JUBALAND
CABINDA
BELGIAN
CONGO
RUANDA
URUNDI
TANGANYIKA
ANGOLA
NORTHERN
RHODESIA
MADAGASCAR
SOUTHERN
RHODESIA
SOUTH
WEST
AFRICA
BECHUANA-
LAND
MOZAMBIQUE
SWAZILAND
UNION OF
SOUTH AFRICA
BASUTOLAND

Poster with General
Paul Emil von
Lettow-Vorbeck on
horseback leading
African soldiers.
The banner reads
Colonial War
Funds. He was
highly respected by
his men, including
his native Askaris.

Germany's overseas empire was dismantled following defeat in the Great War.
With the concluding Treaty of Versailles, German colonies were transformed into
League of Nations mandates and divided between Belgium, the United Kingdom,
certain British Dominions, France and Japan, with a determination not to see any
of them returned to Germany.

Seven days before the Armistice was signed, ending the Great War, the British poet Wilfred Owen was killed in action during a British assault on the Sambre-Oise Canal on the Western Front.

1918
32

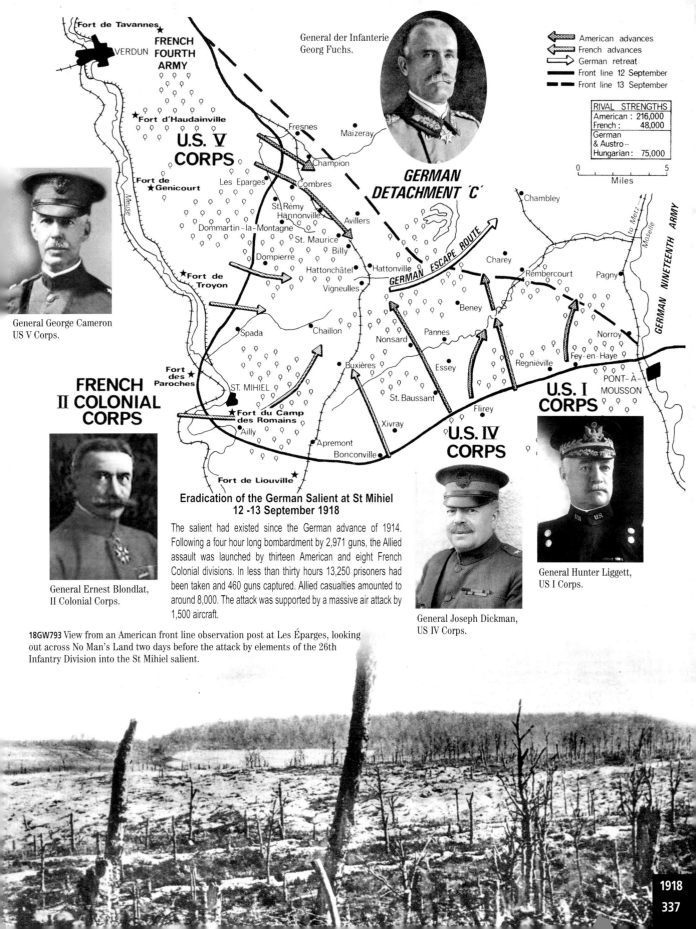

General der Infanterie
Georg Fuchs.

American advances
French advances
German retreat
Front line 12 September
Front line 13 September

RIVAL STRENGTHS	
American :	216,000
French :	48,000
German & Austro-- Hungarian :	75,000

0   5
Miles

Fort de Tavannes
VERDUN
FRENCH FOURTH ARMY
Fort d'Haudainville
U.S. V CORPS
Fort de Genicourt
Les Eparges
Fresnes
Maizeray
Champion
Combres
St Rémy
Hannonville
Avillers
GERMAN DETACHMENT 'C'
Chambley
Dommartin-la-Montagne
St. Maurice
Billy
Dompierre
Hattonchâtel
Hattonville
GERMAN ESCAPE ROUTE
Charey
Rembercourt
Pagny
Fort de Troyon
Vigneulles
Beney
Spada
Chaillon
Nonsard
Pannes
Norroy
Buxières
Essey
Regnièville
Fey-en-Haye
Fort des Paroches
ST. MIHIEL
St. Baussant
Flirey
PONT-À-MOUSSON
U.S. I CORPS
Fort du Camp des Romains
Ailly
Xivray
U.S. IV CORPS
Apremont
Bonconville
Fort de Liouville
GERMAN NINETEENTH ARMY
to Metz
Moselle

General George Cameron
US V Corps.

FRENCH II COLONIAL CORPS

General Ernest Blondlat,
II Colonial Corps.

Eradication of the German Salient at St Mihiel
12 -13 September 1918

The salient had existed since the German advance of 1914. Following a four hour long bombardment by 2,971 guns, the Allied assault was launched by thirteen American and eight French Colonial divisions. In less than thirty hours 13,250 prisoners had been taken and 460 guns captured. Allied casualties amounted to around 8,000. The attack was supported by a massive air attack by 1,500 aircraft.

18GW793 View from an American front line observation post at Les Éparges, looking out across No Man's Land two days before the attack by elements of the 26th Infantry Division into the St Mihiel salient.

General Joseph Dickman,
US IV Corps.

General Hunter Liggett,
US I Corps.

18GW795 Brigadier General Frank Ellis Bamford commanding 2 Brigade, 1st Division, viewing the German held high ground named Mont Sec. When General Pershing first viewed the hill in rising 380 yards above the Woevre lowland he had announced 'We ought to have that mountain'. From Mont Sec the Germans had dominated the entire salient for four years. It took the American IV Army Corps just over twenty-four hours to capture the ground. During the battle the 1st Infantry Division smothered Mont Sec with smoke and the attackers simply went around it.

18GW794 Brigadier General Frank Ellis Bamford with Colonel D K Major outside his HQ in 1918. General Bamford commanded 2 Brigade, 1st Infantry Division.

18GW804, 18GW796, 18GW797. Men of the 1st Infantry Division moving into position for the attack on the St Mihiel salient. Mont Sec can be seen in the distance of the top picture – a strongpoint held by the Germans since 1914.

18GW803 Machine gun battalion of the 18th Infantry Regiment passing through St Baussant for the offensive on the St Mihiel salient.

18GW807, 18GW809.
Fort du Camp des Romains on the summit of Mont Sec and dominating the ground on all sides. This photograph was taken by the US Air Service prior to the attack by IV Corps.

Germans effecting repairs to Fort du Camp des Romains. Note the Gatling style gun dating from the late nineteenth century French defensive armaments and likely no longer operational.

1918
342

18GW813, 18GW811. Entrance to Fort du Camp des Romains in 1918; the date on the gate is 1876 and indicates that the construction followed the Franco-Prussian War of 1870-1871. Barracks within the fort were occupied by German garrison troops.

18GW812 A German officer and NCO stand alongside a collection of Allied shells fired into the fort over four years of occupation that had failed to explode.

18GW810, 18GW808. German officers stand before their shelters, which have been made out of the ruined arches.

18GW812 American artillery men providing the barrage for the St Mihiel offensive. They are operating a French *Canon de 155 C modèle 1917 Schneider*. The United States military decided that the weapon had proven in every way to be superior to all other howitzers of the same or similar calibre. They purchased 1,503 examples of the *Mle 1917* from France and adopted it as the 155 mm Howitzer Carriage, Model of 1917 (Schneider), as the standard howitzer for the United States Army.

18GW815 Men of the 35th Coastal Artillery Company at Baleycourt manning a 340 mm railway gun. The railway gun had a crew of 122 men under the command of Major G F Humbert.

18GW816 Dawn 12 September 1918, American troops passing through the wire with the aid of tank.

18GW806 German machine gun crew on open ground; the Germans were soon having to withdraw as the American assault began to succeed.

18GW818 American infantry attacking through the barbed wire at St Mihiel.

18GW820 A hastily abandoned German machine gun position and the debris left behind.

18GW817 A German 'pillbox' at St Mihiel captured by United States infantry.

18GW826 A group of Doughboys learning their trade during the Battle of St Mihiel.

18GW824 Americans in open country pushing on with their successful break through on the first day of the Battle of St Mihiel.

18GW819 American infantry resting on the first day of the Battle of St Mihiel. They had advanced deep into the German lines.

18GW825 A column of men of the 16th Infantry Regiment trudging towards a bivouac site near St Baussant after their successful action on the 13 September during the Battle of St Mihiel.

18GW821 A captured German concrete pillbox with two American artillery officers siting up on the next target in the Battle of St Mihiel.

18GW822 Some light relief for these Doughboys when a piano was discovered left behind by a rapidly fleeing enemy during the Battle of St Mihiel. An officer knocks out a tune for the benefit of his men. Had the Germans had the time this attractive object could well have been booby-trapped.

18GW827 The destroyed bridge at Flirey, blown up by the French in 1914 to stall the Germn advance. The front line, No Man's Land and German trenches can be seen top right.

18GW829 William M Wright commanded the 89th Infantry Division for the attack on St Mihiel.

18GW828 This point under the blown bridge at Flirey served for a time as headquarters of the 89th Infantry Division during the St Mihiel offensive. It also served as the Field Artillery Brigade HQ during the same engagement.

18GW777 Demonstrating how to care for mules and horses during an enemy gas attack.

18GW833 Germans releasing smoke across the battlefield (they are not wearing respirators, which they would have been had it been poisonous).

18GW834 Gas clouds pouring across No Man's Land.

18GW832 American soldiers donning respirators and firing a rocket to warn of gas clouds coming their way.

18GW835 Americans attacking through gas contaminated air and ground.

18GW830 The 89th Infantry Division commanders had made an error in front of St Mihiel by attempting to hold ground into which a steady bombardment of Mustard gas had been carried out by the Germans. It proved to be costly in casualties to hold. Here medics of the 89th Division treat gas victims in the weeks leading up the American attack.

1918

352

18GW831 Efficient, well trained fighting units gave it their best to effect a breakthrough before the Americans arrived in sufficient numbers and before the newcomers learnt their trade of how to fight a modern war. However, although the Allied line fell back it held and the Americans were quick to learn – the effect was a demoralized German army.

18GW836 Major General Joseph T Dickman, commander of IV Corps (1st, 42nd and 89th Infantry Divisions) during the Battle of St Mihiel.

18GW837 Fighting in the St Mihiel salient, Americans operating a Chauchat machine gun.

18GW798 A column of German prisoners passing along a street in St Mihiel under the watchful eyes of their American captors.

18GW839 This photograph was taken on the afternoon of the first day of the attack on the northern edge of the St Mihiel salient. A tank is being employed as a tractor to haul a trailer of bicycles for army couriers.

18GW838 These German prisoners were captured on the first day of the St Mihiel offensive. Note the American 'western' style covered wagons.

18GW840 The original caption informs us that: *Doughnuts followed the flag very closely. A Salvation Army girl turning them out.*

18GW841 The Americans follow up quickly on their successful breakthrough into the salient.

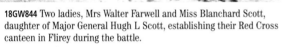

18GW844 Two ladies, Mrs Walter Farwell and Miss Blanchard Scott, daughter of Major General Hugh L Scott, establishing their Red Cross canteen in Flirey during the battle.

18GW843 A Signal Corps field telephone switchboard is being set up after the capture of a German communications centre. In the background is radio equipment bearing the German Imperial arms.

18GW846 Lieutenant Colonel R D Garrett, 42nd Infantry Division, testing a captured field telephone that the Germans did not have time to destroy.

18GW847 Using an American field telephone, an artillery spotter with Battery B, 21st Artillery, 5th Infantry Division sends back range corrections.

18GW845 Hattonchattel, where the American 1st Division and 26th Division effected a juncture early on the second day of the battle. At the time it was realized that the salient was fast disappearing.

18GW851 Officers of the 94th Aero Pursuit Squadron: left is Captain Eddie Rickenbacker, who was becoming the nations's leading air ace, with a final total of twenty-six confirmed victories. In the centre is Lieutenant Douglas Campbell and right, Captain Kenneth Marr.

18GW848 This tank of Company C, 327th Tank Battalion, smashing through wire defences, was driven by Corporal George Heezh.

18GW850 A De Haviland DH4 observing over the St Mihiel salient during the battle.

18GW853 An officer of the 95th Aero Squadron, Lieutenant Buford Jr. This squadron was the first American pursuit squadron to fly in combat on the Western Front.

18GW849 The Becker Type M2 20 mm cannon was a German automatic cannon developed for use in aircraft. This *flugzeugkanone* has been adapted for anti aircraft use and is manned by a crew of three men wearing body armour and gas respirators (1918).

18GW852 American air base at Issoudon, France where many American pilots and observers received their training.

18GW854 American aerial photograph taken of the town of Essey, with the Germans in occupation, August 1918.

18GW855 American aerial view of the ground over which the 89th Infantry Division attacked the German held town of Essey, September 1918.

18GW856 French town's people and refugees in the streets of Essey after the town had been captured by the 89th Infantry Division.

18GW859 In Vigneulles, on a street formly named 'Hindenburgstrasse', these jubilant doughboys, flushed with victory, hold an impromptu renaming ceremony. A significant meeting up of lead elements of the 1st and 26th Infantry Divisions meant that the salient had been eliminated.

18GW857 Some of the first prisoners to be captured by the 103rd Infantry Regiment, 26th Infantry Division early in the attack on the St Mihiel salient.

18GW860 A brief pause in the advance for this supply column gives this supplies officer and his clerks time to catch up with some paperwork before hurrying on behind the infantry.

18GW861, 18GW858. *Weiß dein Mama, dass du raus bist?* A sixteen year old prisoner affords some amusement. Searching the first batch of prisoners for papers and weapons before turning them over to the larger prison camp at Menil-la-Tour. Intelligence officers scrutinize every scrap of paper, private letters and postcards looking for information that might reveal enemy intentions, morale and their supply situation. The stockades were erected several days before the battle in anticipation of a large haul of prisoners.

18GW864 American engineers returning from the front through shell torn Nonsard.

18GW862 During the advance through the crumbling salient these Doughboys take a rest in foxholes dug out of a roadside banking.

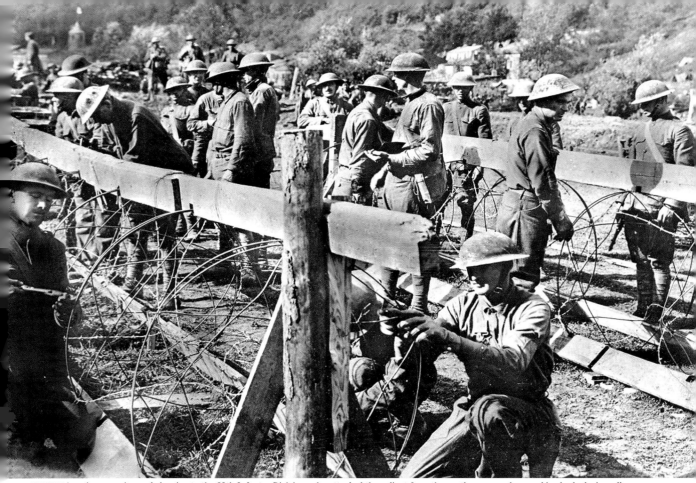

18GW865 Americans engineers belonging to the 89th Infantry Division, who attacked the salient from the south, are seen here making barbed wire rolls on specially constructed wooden frames for use in defence entanglements.

18GW863 An American artillery column hurrying to new firing positions to support the attacking the infantry.

18GW871, 18GW872. Carriages of an American hospital train used to transport wounded of both sides from the Front to base hospitals. Once aboard the specially kitted out carriages, the wounded were effectively in a mobile hospital.

18GW873 The camera has caught happiness and relief on the faces of these slightly wounded men who are telling some fellow soldiers how it happened; one man seems to be displaying paperwork to confirm their stories. Note one of the men sat on the tailboard, with a bandaged left arm, has a cross daubed on his forehead, indicating he is a gas victim. He will be quickly sorted out for appropriate treatment once at the Base hospital.

18GW866 Jubilation is evident among these doughboys as they pose holding captured German weapons and equipment: among the machine guns there is a trench mortar. The St Mihiel battle had been a highly successful operation and the morale of the Americans was, correspondingly, high. They had achieved in their first big engagement what the allied forces had failed to do in four bloody years, driven back the enemy from French soil in such an amazingly short time.

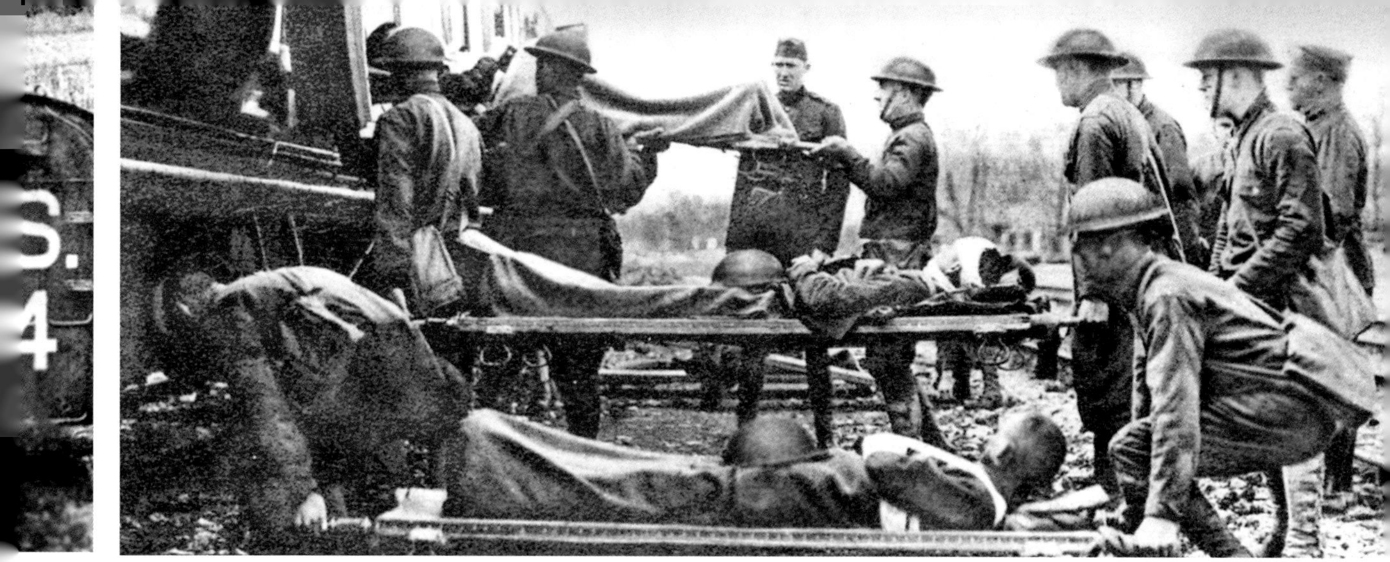

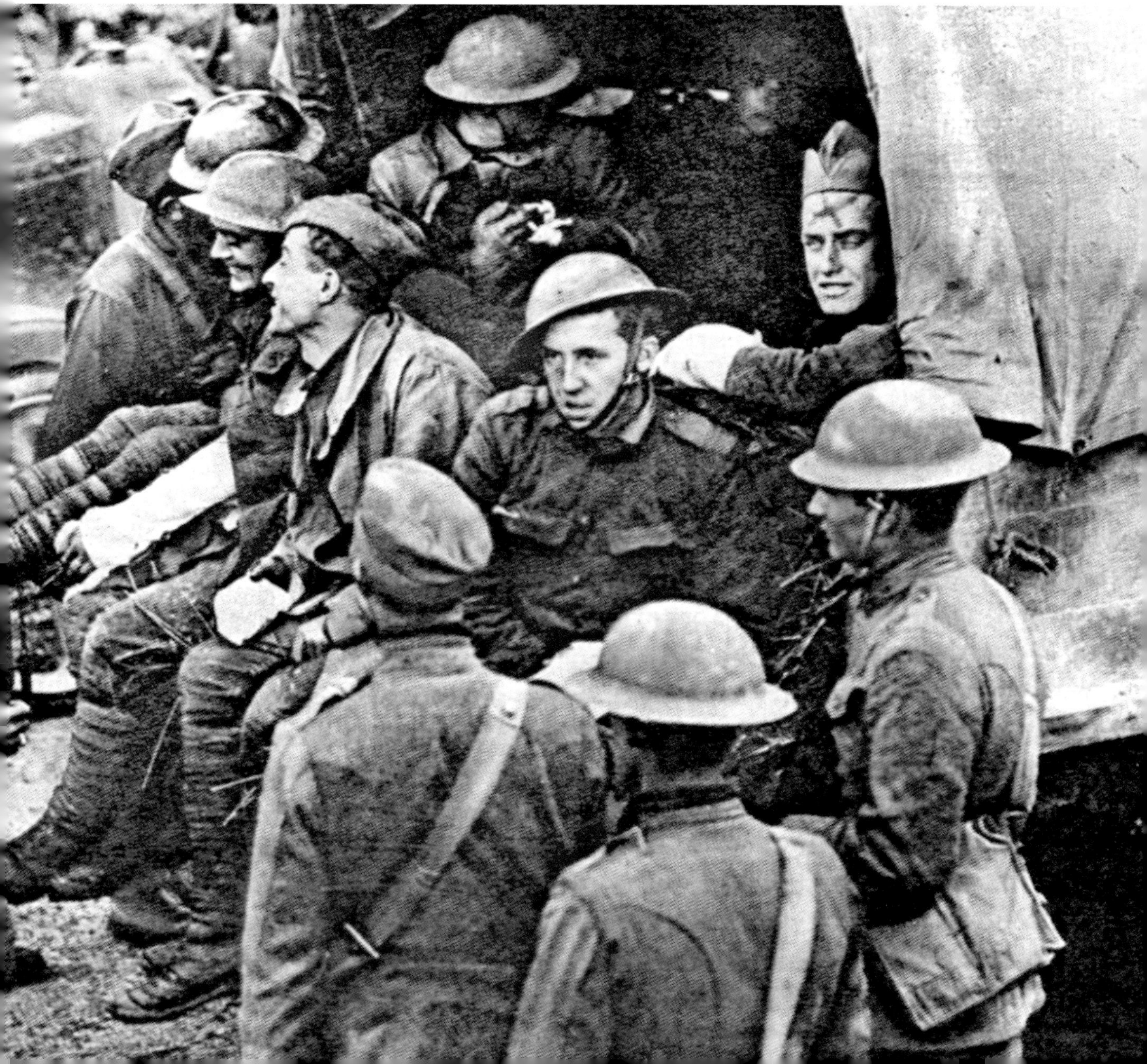

18GW867 Young boys of St Mihiel celebrating their deliverance by the Americans after four years of German occupation.

18GW869 St Mihiel once peace had returned. Not badly damaged compared with Chauvoncourt opposite, across the River Meuse, which was totally destroyed.

18GW870 Another German position taken during the clearing of the St Mihiel salient.

18GW868 When the American advance finally stopped on 15 September 1918, the French town of Thiacourt came to be in the Front Line. The town had been fired by the Germans when they withdrew and bombardment by gas shells became intense; on one night the town was hit by five gas shells a minute for two hours. The French Prime Minister, Raymond Poincaré, along with his wife visited the the town the day of its liberation whilst it was being shelled; such was the relief and delight in having further hectares of their motherland freed.

GENERAL ORDERS No. 238.

It is with soldierly pride that I record in General Orders a tribute to the taking of the St. Mihiel salient by the First Army.

On September 12, 1918, you delivered the first concerted offensive operation of the American Expeditionary Forces upon difficult terrain against this redoubtable position, immovably held for four years, which crumpled before your ably executed advance. Within twenty-four hours of the commencement of the attack, the salient had ceased to exist and you were threatening Metz.

Your divisions, which had never been tried in the exacting conditions of major offensive operations, worthily emulated those of more arduous experience and earned their right to participate in the more difficult task to come. Your staff and auxiliary services, which labored so untiringly and so enthusiastically, deserve equal commendation, and we are indebted to the willing co-operation of the veteran French divisions and of auxiliary units which the Allied commands put at our disposal.

Not only did you straighten a dangerous salient, capture 16,000 prisoners and 443 guns, and liberate 240 square miles of French territory, but you demonstrated the fitness for battle of a unified American army.

We appreciate the loyal training and effort of the First Army. In the name of our country, I offer our hearty and unmeasured thanks to these splendid Americans of the I, IV and V Corps and of the 1st, 2nd, 4th, 5th, 26th, 42nd, 82nd, 89th and 90th Divisions, which were engaged, and of the 3rd, 35th, 78th, 80th and 91st Divisions, which were in reserve.

JOHN J. PERSHING,
General, Commander in Chief

18GW823 General John J Pershing and commander of the 1st Infantry Division and V Corps, Major General Charles P. Summerall, are looking obviously pleased in this photograph and with good reason, the American Expeditionary Force had acquitted itself well and a national army had emerged that would soon equal that of any major european power.

18GW824 General John J Pershing with French politicians and generals reviewing American troops.

Following the American Expeditionary Force's success in eliminating the St Mihiel salient, the next step was for the Americans to take over a portion of the Western Front. On 6 August 1918, Foch was made a Marshal of France. Along with the British commander, Field Marshal Sir Douglas Haig, Foch planned the Grand Offensive, opening on 26 September 1918, which led to the defeat of Germany. The strategic plan agreed upon by the Allied commanders involved an offensive along the entire Western Front from the River Meuse to the English Channel. The Americans would make their effort astride the Meuse, thrusting through the Argonne region in the direction of Sedan-Mezières, by the French and British north towards Cambrai-St Quentin and by the British and Belgians in Flanders.

18GW825 Marshal Ferdinand Foch was appointed Supreme Commander of all the Allied forces in Europe.

18GW876 Men of the 132nd Infantry Regiment, 33rd Infantry Division, III Corps, in trenches north of Verdun, 17 March 1918. From this position could be viewed the valley of the River Meuse and the ground over which the 33rd Division would attack on 26 September. Following a six hour bombardment, nine American infantry divisions would advance against German positions in the Argonne Forest and along the Meuse River. The 132nd Infantry Regiment was descended from two formations of the Union Army from the American Civil War: the Montgomery Guards and Colonel James A Mulligan's 23rd Illinois Volunteers (or Irish Brigade). Note the soldier pretending to pull the safety pin on a grenade.

18GW877 French Renault light tanks with American crews of 326th Battery, 311th Tank Center, moving up to their places ready for the forthcoming attack.

18GW878 United States Secretary of War, Newton D Baker, and Major General J W McAndrew observe the cross examination of a captured German officer by intelligence officers 1st Lieutenant Jennings and 2nd Lieutenant McCoy. Information acquired through interrogation would greatly assist in the coming attack.

18GW879 The 326th Tank Battery trundling up to jump off positions near Boureuilles 26 September 1918.

18GW880 TA Spad two seater from an American squadron on a reconnaissance flight over German positions prior to the attack.

18GW884 Men of the 28th Division, 103rd Engineers, companies A and E, repairing the blown bridge at Boureuilles, destroyed by the Germans.

18GW883 A 340 mm gun manned by the US Coast Guard Artillery Corps firing shells into the German lines from the area of Nixeville, 24 September 1918.

18GW881 American and French troops and equipment packing the roads near Esnes before the Meuse-Argonne offensive.

18GW882 American observation balloon with an artillery spotter in the basket. A telephone line led direct to his gun battery for making shot corrections. Enemy troop movements were also reported and hence balloons on both sides were a prime target for aircraft attack; balloons were kept well defended by anti-aircraft guns.

ARMY GROUP RUPPRECHT
Crown Prince of Bavaria

ARMY GROUP GALLWITZ
Max von Gallwitz

to Sedan

Dun-sur-Meuse

——— Allied front line 26 September 1918.
– – – U.S. First Army's objective.
▲▲▲ U.S. First Army's front line 30 September 19
– × – Army boundaries.
ọ ọ Forests.

GERMAN FIFTH ARMY

Damvillers

Aisne

Fleville

GERMAN
I RESERVE

GERMAN
GEN KDO
58

Apremont

Montfaucon

GERMAN V RESERVE

GERMAN XXI

Beaumont

AUSTRIAN
XVIII

Varennes

FRENCH XVII

FRENCH
XXXVIII

Forêt

Avocourt

III CORPS

Vienne

I CORPS

V CORPS

Verdun

Dombasle

0   Miles   5

FRENCH
FOURTH ARMY

AMERICAN   FIRST   ARMY

Meuse

When the American First
Army attacked at St Mihiel
on 12 September 1918, the
Germans had decided to
abandon the salient and
were preparing to withdraw.
The result was the
Americans took 16,000
prisoners at a cost of only
7,000 casualties. A United
States National Army had
been forged; however, for
the Meuse-Argonne
offensive overconfidence
was evident in the planning.

Hunter Liggett
I CORPS

George Cameron
V CORPS

Robert Lee Bullard
III CORPS

*No commander was ever privileged to lead a finer force; no commander
ever derived greater inspiration from the performance of his troops.*

— John J. Pershing

FOR THE MEUSE-ARGONNE OFFENSIVE General Pershing and his staff assigned the assaulting divisions a ten mile penetration for the
first day, 26 September, punching through two German defence lines. The terrain was different to that of St Mihiel, it was heavily wooded
and the Germans had every reason to put up a strong resistance as their supply railway system which lay behind them sustained the entire
front. Of the nine assaulting American divisions, only the 4th, 28th, 33rd and 77th had seen action over the spring and summer months when
they assisted in repulsing the German offensives. Two American divisions, the 79th and 91st, had never served in the front lines.

III CORPS

George Bell
33rd Division
Illinois N Guard
Prairie Division
129th, 130th, 131st, 132nd Infantry
122nd, 123rd, 124th Artillery
122nd, 123rd, 124th Machine Gun
108th Engineers

Adelbert Cronkhite
80th Division
Virginia N Army
Blue Ridge Division
317th, 318th, 319th, 320th Infantry
313th, 314th, 315th Artillery
313th, 314th, 315th Machine Gun
305th Engineers

John L. Hines
4th Division
Regular Army
Ivy Division
39th, 47th, 58th, 59th Infantry
13th, 16th, 77th Artillery
10th, 11th, 12th Machine Gun
4th Engineers

Preston Brown
3rd Division
Regular Army
Marne Division
4th, 7th, 30th, 38th Infantry
10th, 18th, 76th Artillery
7th, 8th, 9th Machine Gun
6th Engineers

Charles P. Summerall
1st Division
Regular Army
The Big Red One Division
16th, 18th, 26th, 28th Infantry
5th, 6th, 7th Artillery
1st, 2nd, 3rd Machine Gun
1st Engineers

V CORPS

Joseph E. Kuhn
79th Division
National Army
Lorraine Division
313th, 314th, 315th, 316th Infantry
310th, 311th, 312th Artillery
310th, 311th, 312th Machine Gun
304th Engineers

Charles Farnsworth
37th Division
Ohio N Guard
Buckeye Division
145th, 146th, 147th, 148th Infantry
134th, 135th, 136th Artillery
134th, 135th, 136th Machine Gun
112th Engineers

W H Johnston
91st Division
Regular Army
Wild West Division
361st, 362nd, 363rd, 364th Infantry
346th, 347th, 348th Artillery
346th, 347th, 348th Machine Gun
316th Engineers

William G Haan
32nd Division
Wisconsin/Michigan NG
Red Division
125th, 126th, 127th, 128th Infantry
119th, 120th, 121st Artillery
119th, 120th, 121st Machine Gun
107th Engineers

Charles L Morton
29th Division
NJ/Delaware/Maryland NG
Blue & Grey Division
113th, 114th, 115th, 116th Infantry
110th, 111th, 112th Artillery
110th, 111th, 112th Machine Gun
104th Engineers

I CORPS

Peter E Traub
35th Division
Missouri/Kansas N Guard
Santa Fe Division
137th, 138th, 139st, 140th Infantry
128th, 129th, 130th Artillery
128th, 129th, 130th Machine Gun
110th Engineers

Charles Henry Muir
28th Division
Pennsylvania N Guard
Keystone Division
109th, 110th, 111th, 112th Infantry
107th, 108th, 109th Artillery
107th, 108th, 109th Machine Gun
103rd Engineers

Robert Alexander
77th Division
Regular Army
Statue of Liberty Division
305th, 306th, 307th, 308th Infantry
304th, 305th, 306th Artillery
304th, 305th, 306th Machine Gun
302nd Engineers

Charles C Ballou
92nd Division
(Negroes) Regular Army
Buffalo Division
366th, 367th, 368th Infantry
349th, 350th, 351st Artillery
349th, 350th, 351st Machine Gun
317th Engineers

George B Duncan
82nd Division
Regular Army
All American Division
325th, 326th, 327th, 328th Infantry
319th, 320th, 321st Artillery
319th, 320th, 321st Machine Gun
307th Engineers

18GW904 Commander of the 80th Infantry Division, III Corps, Major General Cronkhite, discusses their objectives with his Chief of Staff, Colonel Waldron.

18GW905 A French map, with the situation marked up, supplied to the Americans by their ally.

18GW906 Commander of I Corps, Lieutenant General Hunter Liggett was noted for his detailed preparation, which was evident in the great care he took in preparing his divisions for operations. A map of the Argonne is on the wall behind him.

SITUATION des FORCES ENNEMIES.

DEVANT LE FRONT DU 17ᵉ C.A.

Le 12 Sepᵇʳᵉ 1918.

EN BLEU: Déplacements contrôlés après le 12 Sepᵇʳᵉ.

18GW911 The French town of Souilly, headquarters of General John J Pershing at the beginning of the greatest test of American forces, which involved the employment of 1,200,000 men, the use of 2,417 guns and 4,214,000 rounds of artillery ammunition. General Pershing's office was in the mairie (town hall) from where General Pétain had directed the the defence of Verdun.

18GW914 The commander-in-chief, General Pershing, seen here on one of his regular trips to the front lines. According to the Signal Corps caption he is discussing some of the problems the 91st Infantry Division (the 'Wild West' Division) is experiencing with its commander, Major General William H Johnston.

18GW915 18GW916 The commander of the 37th Infantry Division (Ohio National Guard), Major General Charles Farnsworth, consults a map the day before the attack.

Men of the 112th Engineers Battalion, 37th Infantry Division, eating a meal before they advance; Avocourt, 26 September.

18GW913 Bringing forward artillery pieces – French 75s – to the forest of the Argonne near Nixeville; this unit is the 313th Field Artillery, supporting the 80th Infantry Division.

18GW909 Holding the pivotal position on the west bank of the Meuse river opposite Consenvoye are these men of the Illinois National Guard, the 132nd Infantry Regiment, 33nd Infantry Division. The division held the position for seven days, 27 September to 4 October, before making the crossing.

18GW907 Men of the 2nd Battalion, 307th Infantry Regiment, 77th Infantry Division (nicknamed 'Statue of Liberty Division'), I Corps, seen assembled one and a half miles behind their start line and awaiting orders to move forward. Note some have opted to fix bayonets – perhaps for the Signal Corps cameraman.

18GW912 The edge of the Argonne Forest where the 35th Infantry Division, ('Santa Fe Division') the Missouri and Kansas National Guard, commanded by General Traub attacked at dawn 26 September 1918. Along the front 250,000 men went forward into a dense ground fog and were expected to advance ten miles over the ridges, clearing the enemy from the forest of the Argonne and bursting through two of the three German defence lines.

18GW917 Yanks streaming through the recently captured French town of Varennes, taken on the first day of the Meuse-Argonne offensive by the 28th and 35th Infantry Divisions.

18GW918, 18GW924 A battery of 155 mm howizers in the ruins of the town of Varennes. The original caption reads: *...helping to speed the enemy on his way.*

18GW919 Major General Peter Traub, commanding the 35th Infantry Division, outside his HQ. The original caption informs us: *Both he and Major Cordiner, to whom he is talking, are in combat equipment. General Traub is carrying an old type gas mask while Major Cordiner is carrying the new respirator, slung on his back.*

18GW921 Battery C, 108th Field Artillery, 28th Infantry Division, firing on the withdrawing Germans from the ruins of Varennes.

18GW910 Varennes was taken on the first day of the battle by regiments of the 28th and 35th Infantry Divisions. The original caption reads: *Probably few of the Pennsylvania and Missouri National Guardsmen of those divisions knew that 127 years ago Louis XVI and Marie Antoinette were arrested here and taken back to Paris and the guillotine.*

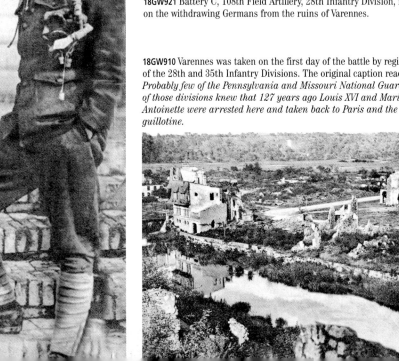

1918
389

18GW927 Men of the 130th Ambulance Company, 108th Sanitary Corps, 33rd infantry Division, transporting wounded on stretcher carts

18GW923 German prisoners under escort assisting a wounded Yank during the first day of the American attack.

18GW920 Their first objective taken, members of Company B, 108th Machine Gun Battalion, 28th Infantry Division, are halted and resting near Boureuilles.

18GW922 Three Doughboys, not dead, just exhausted after a hard first day of fighting.

18GW925 Major General H Muir, commanding 28th Infantry Division.

18GW926 One man keeps on the watch as his buddies grab some sleep in this captured trench in the German second line during the first day's advance. They are men of the 308th Infantry Regiment, 77th Infantry Division.

18GW935 The Germans were evicted by the 77th Infantry Division from their four years' comfortable occupancy of these dugouts in the Argonne Forest.

18GW934 Two Americans have just been wounded, Sergeant George Norman and a buddy from Company C, 308th Infantry Regiment, 77th Infantry Division, and are being taken to a dressing station.

18GW937 Officers have used abandoned German steins for this posed photograph of happy, drinking conquerors. One of them, however, is a 'dry' member of the State of Georgia Prohibitionalists and is helping the cameraman by pretending.

18GW936 Major General Robert Alexander, commanding the 77th Infantry Division.

18GW938 Domesticity in the Argonne Forest, a Yank makes repairs to his clothing with a needle and thread.

'It is again impressed upon every officer and man of this command that ground once captured must under no circumstances be given up in the absence of direct, positive, and formal orders to do so emanating from these headquarters. Troops occupying ground must be supported against counterattack and all gains held. It is a favorite trick of the Boche to spread confusion…by calling out 'retire' or 'fall back'. If, in action, any such command is heard, officers and men may be sure that it is given by the enemy. Whoever gives such a command is a traitor and it is the duty of any officer or man who is loyal to his country and who hears such an order given to shoot the offender upon the spot. WE ARE NOT GOING BACK BUT FORWARD!
–General Alexander

18GW940 The original title reads: *Dreaming of home. Men of the 77th Infantry Division in a deserted house in Cornay.*

18GW945 Sergeant Hussey leading a patrol in the Argonne Forest. A dead German lies in the foreground.

The Lost Battalion

At dawn 2 October, 1918, the 77th Division was ordered to advance against the German line as part of a large American attack in the Meuse-Argonne. Major Charles Whittlesey commanded a mixed battalion of 554 men, who advanced forward through a ravine. Because the units on their flanks failed to make headway, Whittlesey's troops became cut off and pinned down by machine gun and rifle fire from the surrounding high ground. The following four days were perilous for Whittlesey and his men, as they were without food or water. They resisted numerous attacks on their perimeter and on one occasion the Germans tried flame throwers to break through. During this period war correspondents dubbed the unit the 'Lost Battalion'. On the 7 October, the Germans sent forward a blindfolded American PoW carrying a white flag, with a message in English:

> The suffering of your wounded men can be heard over here in the German lines, and we are appealing to your humane sentiments to stop. A white flag shown by one of your men will tell us that you agree with these conditions. Please treat Private Lowell R. Hollingshead [the bearer] as an honorable man. He is quite a soldier. We envy you. The German commanding officer.

Whittlesey made no reply. He ordered white sheets that had been placed as signals for Allied aircraft to drop supplies to be pulled in so they would not be mistaken for surrender signals. That night, a relief force arrived and the Germans withdrew. Of the original 554 troops involved in the advance, 107 had been killed, 63 were missing and 190 were wounded. Only 194 were able to walk out of the ravine.

18GW944 Major Charles Whittlesey commander of the 'Lost Battalion' and Major McKinney commander of the 3rd Battalion, 307th Infantry Regiment. The 3rd relieved the isolated and cut off unit. Major Whittlesey received the Congressional Medal of Honor. His citation reads in part:

Although cut off for five days from the remainder of his division, Major Whittlesey maintained the position which he had reached under orders for an advance and held his command, originally consisting of 463 officers and men, together in the face of superior numbers of the enemy for five days. Major Whittlesey and his command were thus cut off and no rations or other supplies reached him in spite of determind efforts which were made by the division. On the fourth day Major Whittlesey received from the enemy a written proposition to surrender which he treated with contempt, although at the time he was out of rations and had suffered a loss of about fifty per cent killed and wounded of his command and was surrounded by the enemy.
He committed suicide in 1921.

18GW943 All that remained of the so-called 'Lost Battalion' of the 77th Infantry Division after having been cut off by the Germans for five days. About seven companies of the 308th and 307th Infantry Regiments became cut off on the La Viergette road about 500 meters east of the Moulin de Charlevaux, in the heart of the Argonne. The Germans filtered in behind the seven companies led by Major Charles Whittlesey and cut them off. It was finally rescued by the 3rd Battalion, 307th Infantry Regiment, under the command of Major McKinney

18GW947 Captain Alexander Reves Skinker Company I, 138th Infantry Regiment, 35th Division, killed in action at Cheppy, France, September 26, 1918; posthumously award the Medal of Honor.

Citation: *Unwilling to sacrifice his men when his company was held up by terrific machinegun fire from iron pill boxes in the Hindenburg Line, Captain Skinker personally led an automatic rifleman and a carrier in an attack on the machine guns. The carrier was killed instantly, but Captain Skinker seized the ammunition and continued through an opening in the barbed wire, feeding the automatic rifle until he, too, was killed.*

18GW946 A section of the battlefield near Vauquois Hill, where intensive underground mining operations had taken place between the French and Germans before the Americans fought here in September 1918. The official caption for this picture reads: *The desperate bravery of the Missourians at Vauquois and Cheppy was one of the outstanding features of the first phase of the Meuse-Argonne operations.* The large overlapping mine craters are in No Man's Land and German troops can be seen manning the trenches.

18GW928 The original title reads: *Poilu of the 320th Regiment, Fourth French Army and doughboys of the 312th Infantry Regiment, 78th Infantry Division, advanced northwards together.*

18GW929 The original title reads: *Sergeant J W Killigrow, 78th Division pals with the children of Authe.*

18GW932 Seen here transporting water and food to the front line is this infantryman and his donkey of the 132nd Infantry Regiment, 33rd Infantry Division, September 1918.

18GW931 Liberated after four years of occupation; Chaplain Jackson, 78th Infantry Division, fits a pair of old issue shoes on a French child at Brieulles-sur-Bar.

18GW941 Bringing in German prisoners. The original caption: *26,000 Germans cried 'Kamerad' during the operations of the American First Army in the Meuse-Argonne sector.*

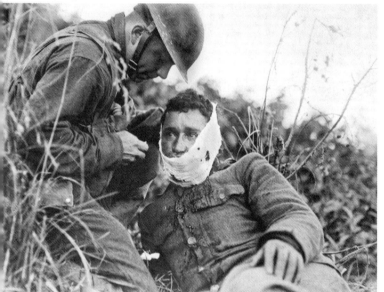

18GW948 A doughboy has just been shot through the jaw and receives first-aid from a concerned buddy.

18GW942 'German wounded received scrupulous care' the original caption says. German stretcher bearers carry a fellow soldier.

18GW939 American walking wounded look on from their transport: *with grim satisfaction as a file of German prisoners pass.* (Original caption).

18GW951 A first aid dressing station near Nantillois.

18GW952 A large number of *Landsturm* troops were encountered by the 77th Infantry Division in the Argonne. These second class troops were usually employed in activities behind the front line.

18GW953 Machine gunners firing at a German plane flying over Cunel.

18GW954 A German Hannover C.L. III A 3892/18 brought down in the Argonne by American machine gunners, between Montfaucon and Cierges. Red Crosses were painted on wings and fuselage (October 1918).

18GW955, 18GW956. To illustrate the spirit of the time the original caption for these pictures is as follows: *German propaganda, one of Ludendorf's own specialities, caused the debacle of Cadorna's army in Italy in 1917. It is said to have contributed to the defeat of Gough's Fifth Army on the British front in 1918, but all it got from our soldiers was raucous laughter. The picture on the left shows a German 'hot air' balloon that was wafted over our lines and fell at Sommedieue 28 October.*
Left to right are Lt Kenneth G Lewis, Major Milton McLean and Sergeant N B Waugh. Below is a reproduction of one of the leaflets the balloon dropped.

Life, Liberty and Happiness.

So long as the Administration is determined to keep the war going there is only one way for you to get out of this miserable fix and that is for you to stop fighting. As a free born American citizen you do this honourably. You can have the right to

life, liberty and the pursuit of happiness.
The American constitution guarantees to you these rights. **Exercise them!**

Get out and dash to safety! If you don't, you stand a very slim chance of ever seeing Broadway or the old home again. The Wall Street millionaires may like this war, because they are becoming billionaires. But you will have to pay for it all, my boy,

pay for it with your blood and taxes
and the tears of your loved ones at home.

If you were fighting on your own soil against a foreign foe it would be another matter, but what are you doing in Europe? France is not your country, neither is Belgium nor Alsace Lorraine. Are you satisfied that you are in the full enjoyment of your "inalienable rights to life, liberty and the pursuit of happiness" as promised to you by the

American bill of rights.

The years will be lean and weary and the work will be hard and long for you and the longer the war lasts the longer will be the debt which you will have to pay to the money magnates of Wall Street for the munitions you are shooting away.

Don't give up your life till you have to and don't give any more labor for the **benefit of the money trust!** Quit it!

———— ❧ ————

1918
402

18GW961 American support troops running to supply and reinforce the assaulting battalion October 1918.

18GW960, 18GW959, 18GW958. Gathering together the human debris of the battle, both American and German dead, for identification and burial.

18GW957 The ground over which 328th Infantry Regiment of the 82nd Infantry Division, (All American), advanced in its attack on Hill 223 near Chatel Chéhéry, 8 October 1918. It was here that Alvin C York carried out the action that was to earn him the title of the 'greatest individual fighter of the war'.

18GW969 Injured men of the 2nd Battalion, 326th Infantry Regiment, 82nd Infantry Division, at a roadside in the Argonne, awaiting transport to remove them for treatment for poison gas contamination.

18GW966 Major General George B Duncan, commander of 82nd Infantry Division.

A Tennessee mountain man, Corporal Alvin York, Company G, 328th Infantry Regiment, 82nd Infantry Division, became a legend in a remarkable action which won him the Medal of Honor. From childhood he had grown up with a hunting rifle in his hands and could knock the head off a turkey at 100 yards. When his company's advance was stopped by German machine guns on a hill ahead of them, Corporal York worked his way through the woods into the German rear with sixteen other men. They captured the commander of the machine gun battalion, however, fire from the hill killed half of York's men and pinned down the rest. With his rifle and automatic pistol, York 'hunted' and killed twenty-eight Germans with the most accurate of calculated shots. Realizing they were up against a relentless and deady marksman the German officer suddenly blew his whistle and ordered his men to lay down their arms. York promptly marched the prisoners back to the American lines, scooping up more prisoners along the way, to bring his total bag to over 132, this included four officers. In addition, thirty-five machine guns were captured.

18GW967 Corporal Alvin C York – later sergeant – at the place where he systematically began picking off twenty of the enemy with rifle and pistol. As an elder in a Tennessee mountain church at the beginning of the war, he was a conscientious objector, but then changed his mind to become the most efficient of killers.

The Congressional Medal of Honor citation reads: *After his platoon suffered heavy casualties and three other noncommissioned officers had become casualties, Corporal York assumed command. Fearlessly leading seven men, he charged with great daring a machine gun nest which was pouring deadly and incessant fire upon his platoon. In this heroic feat the machine gun nest was taken, together with four officers and 128 men and several guns.*

18GW965 German machine gun teams operating the MG 08 heavy machine guns.

18GW962, 18GW963. Men of the 315th Machine Gun Battalion, 80th Infantry Division, 'Blue Ridge Division', Virginia National Army, advancing and setting up machine guns in the Argonne Forest, October 1918. Their weapons are water-cooled Browning M1917 heavy machine guns.

18GW970 A French Breguet 14 bomber aircraft at the United States Army Air Service Production Center No. 2, Romorantin Aerodrome, France, 1918. Following successful deployment by the French, the type was ordered by the United States Army Air Service (over 600 aircraft). By the end of the First World War 5,500 Breguet 14s had been produced.

18GW971 A Breguet bomber; the original caption reads: *While the ground soldiers were pushing back the Germans through the Argonne, bombing planes went forth each night to increase the enemy troubles. These bombers destroyed* [attacked] *railway lines, supply bases and munition dumps behind the lines.*

18GW975 Pilots of 94th Aero Squadron at Rembercourt Aerodrome, France, November 1918.

18GW976 Edward Vernon Rickenbacker in the cockpit of his Spad XIII.

18GW974 Pilots of 94th Aero Squadron at Foucaucourt aerodrome, France, November 1918. They are: 1st Leutenant Reed Chambers, Captain James Meissner, 1st Leutenant Eddie Rickenbacker,1st Leutenant T C Taylor and 1st Leutenant J H Eastman.

18GW973 Eddie Rickenbacker shot down his first enemy aircraft on the 29 April, 1918. The following month he claimed his fifth kill to become an ace. By November he had claimed further victories bringing his final total to twenty-six, becoming America's leading ace

18GW978 'Big Nims' of the 3rd Battalion, 366th Infantry Regiment, 92nd Infantry Division, finds great amusement at the grotesque appearance of a buddy with a gas mask over his face.

18GW977 Negro infantrymen of the 92nd Infantry Division advancing in file along a road in the Argonne. The road has been camouflaged by engineers to hide troop movements from the Germans.

The 92nd Infantry Division, a military unit of approximately twenty thousand officers and men, was one of only two all-black divisions to fight in the United States Army in the First World War. After their arrival in France, the soldiers were deployed to the front lines in August 1918. The division saw action in the Meuse-Argonne offensive. The 92nd Division, unlike the 93rd, the other all-black division in France, fought under American command. The Americans were reluctant to employ the 93rd Infantry Division, regarding it to be inferior in fighting quality and white officers did not want to command them. The French had no such hesitation. They welcomed the 93rd and assigned its four regiments to three French divisions where they wore American uniforms but ate French food, used French equipment and fought using French tactics.

18GW979 Men of the 93rd Infantry Division; their regiments were integrated into the French infantry divisions and the men responded well to their French officers and a number of gallantry medals were awarded.

18GW972 A place where death lurked at every bend: a captured section of the much deteriorated Varenne-Four de Paris road in the Argonne forest; at the time used as a supply track for German artillery positions. Signs on the trees are German notices indicating where ammunition dumps are located.

18GW980 Boobytraps and mantraps lay hidden to catch the unwary along the forest trails and paths of the Argonne.

18GW981 German snipers operating in the thick forest.

18GW982 A woodland cemetery in the heart of the Argonne forest.

18GW983 Men of the 18th Infantry Regiment, 1st Infantry Division (The Big Red One) in shallow fox holes during an attack on a German position.

18GW984 Three-man crew using a 37 mm gun against German pill boxes. This weapon was less effective than a mortar and was discontinued after the war.

18GW1021 A happy time for these men of the Headquarters Company, 312th Infantry Regiment, 78th Infantry Division, as some appear to have just received letters from the folks back home.

18GW1017 A German machine gunner's view of the Valley of the Aire. The entire strongpoint on this hillside bristled with machine guns, which poured murderous fire into the attacking Americans as they advanced down the valley of the Aire. The postion was captured after three attempts. A Doughboy squints along the line of fire. Note the pile of spent cartridge cases.

18GW1015 Men of the 42nd Infantry Division moving along the Imecourt road to take part in the final part of the Meuse-Argonne operations pass evidence of the desperate resistance the Germans were making. In the foreground is the crew of a Maxim machine gun killed at their post, 4 November 1918.

18GW1019 With shells bursting across a hillside near Exermont American Signal Corps cameraman, Captain Nicholas McDonald, cranked his movie camera and produced 600 feet of a battle in progress. A battery of the 6th Field Artillery is taking a pasting from German guns and was forced to withdraw.

18GW1020 The original caption for the lone soldier: *The terrific punishment sustained by the men of the 4th Division during their advance in the Meuse-Argonne is planly written in the drawn features of... Corporal Erland Johnson, Company L, 58th Infantry Regiment.*

18GW1018 Two machine gunners of the 90th Infantry Division, Glen Haskin and Alfred Wolf, operating a British manufactured Vickers machine gun in the Bois des Rappes in support of the 358th Infantry Regiment.

18GW1016 The body of a German machine gunner beside his now silent weapon on the Hindenburg Line, who carried out his orders to hold up the American advance to the end.

18GW985 A sniper with telescopic-sighted rifle and a machine gunner covering the withdrawal of German forces in the Argonne region, late October 1918.

18GW986 German troops retreating towards the German border in November 1918.

18GW989,18GW990. Street scene in the town of Exermont, which has just been occupied by men of the 1st Infantry Division. The Division had been in continuous action during an advance of seven kilometers along the Aire valley and casualties in the period were 8,500. When these two photographs were taken the Germans began shelling the village and men, who moments before had been strolling the street suddenly had to race for cover. Note the dead German lying on the road.

18GW995 Three wounded German prisoners are the centre of attention as they receive first aid.

18GW993 With the German occupiers on the run after four years, French and Belgian civilians could begin moving back into their property. These Doughboys are in hot pursuit.

Henry Nicholas John Gunther (June 6, 1895 – November 11, 1918) is believed to be the last soldier of any of the belligerents to be killed during the First World War. He was killed at 10.59 am, one minute before the Armistice was to take effect at 11 am. Gunther's squad approached a roadblock of two German machine guns in the village of Chaumont-devant-Damvillers, Lorraine. Gunther carried out a lone bayonet charge. The Germans were aware of the Armistice that would take effect in one minute's time and tried to wave Gunther off. However, he kept going and fired a shot or two. When he got too close to the machine guns, he was shot in a short burst of fire and killed instantly.

Gunther's remains were returned to the United States in 1923 and buried at the Most Holy Redeemer Cemetery in Baltimore.

18GW1013 'Corpus Christi; Sanguis Christi': Roman Catholic Chaplain A L Girard, 108th Sanitary Train, 33rd Infantry Division, conducting Mass for men of his unit. He was curate at the Church of St Thomas the Apostle, Chicago. The belief that human sacrifice in battle could be equated to that of the Christ was constantly reinforced by chaplains on both sides. The service took place in a shell wrecked church in the wake of the retreating Germans.

18GW1014 Jewish soldiers attending a religious service at Chaumont, American Expeditionary Force General Headquarters. The French officer, wearing a beard on the left, is Captain A Levy, Mayor of Chaumont; his wife is sitting next to him. Next to her is Rabbi Jacob Kohn of New York City. Unlike those professing the Christian belief, they are still awaiting their Messiah to make an appearance; consequently they are not conducting themselves in contradiction of the direction to love their enemies.

18GW1011 A ceremony on 13 November 1918 to honour the dead of the 79th Division killed in repeated charges against innumerable machine guns on Hill 378 (Borne de Cornouiller – 'Corn Willy'). The assault had begun at Molleville Farm and that is where the dead were buried.

18GW1010 Graves at Cheveuges of the last Americans to be killed in front of Sedan. There was a drive among some American commanders to be first to capture the prize of the city. However, the Supreme Allied Commander, Marshal Foch, halted the Americans so that a French division should have the privilege. Note the rifles laid on each grave – not a practice that would have any permanency, nor the steel helmets hung over the names. It would probably have been done for a religious ceremony conducted at the cemetery.

18GW999 Colonel Henry J Reilly, commander of 83 Brigade, which comprised 165th and 166th Infantry Regiments, 42nd Infantry Division. The other brigade in the division was 84 Brigade, which comprised the 167th and 168th Infantry Regiments.

18GW998 Men of the 166th Infantry Regiment, (part of the Ohio National Guard) resting on front of Cheveuges, near Sedan, 9 November 1918. From the hill in the background the King of Prussia William 1 watched the Battle of Sedan forty-eight years previously. A French division had been given the privilege of capturing Sedan.

18GW1001 With hours left to go before signing of the armistice, a youngster helps clean up some doughboys by manning the village pump at Raucourt.

18GW1000 Major General William M Wright and officers of the 89th Infantry Division who fought to the eleventh hour of the eleventh month despite an armistice being signed at 5 am on the morning of 11 November 1918. The two other senior officers are: Major General Frank L Winn and Brigadier General Henry D Todd.

18GW1002 A First Aid Post in Remonville with an ammunition wagon of the 89th Division passing through the make-shift barracades, 2 November 1918. The war has just over a week to go.

18GW991 A street in Thelonne in the Ardennes. Soldiers of the 16th Infantry Regiment, 1st Infantry Division, take down some information from a local woman. The 'Big Red One' was pushing at speed to capture the city of Sedan, situated on the border of France as this would be a significant prize for the commanding general. However, in the race were five other American divisions and one French. On 7 November Marshal Foch ordered the American divisions to halt; the French would have the honour to take Sedan.

18GW992 The Château de Sedan dominating the city. From January 1917 until November 1918 it was used as a prison, called 'the Penal Colony' by the Sedan people, where both French and Belgians were interned for resisting work in the labour battalions (*ZivilArbeiter Bataillon*). In the occupied zones, civilians from 14 to 60 years old were requisitioned. During the Franco-Prussian War of 1870-1871 French emperor Napoleon III was taken prisoner along with 100,000 of his soldiers at the First Battle of Sedan and for the French to recapture the border town forty years later was to be a major event.

18GW949 Two more minutes to fight: a detachment of the 89th Infantry Division shelter behind a flimsy barricade thrown up by the defenders near the church in the town of Stenay. The time was 10.58, on the 11 November 1918 – the Great War had two minutes left before the armistice and an official cease fire. They had suffered many casualties that morning, including sixty-one killed. After 11 am they could have walked in and taken the town for no loss of life but their divisional commander, Major General Wright, ordered his men to fight to the final minute.

18GW829 Major General William M Wright commanded the 89th Infantry Division and went ahead with an attack on the town of Stenay only hours before the armistice was to take effect. There were 365 casualties, including 61 dead. They could have walked into the town with no casualties after 11 am.

18GW829 Major General Charles Pelot Summerall commanded V Corps from 13 October 1918 to the end of the war. He ordered the US Marines to cross the River Meuse on the 10th/11th November. They took 1,100 casualties. In a few hours they could have crossed the river unhindered and with no casualties.

I intend to pursue the Feldgrauen [field greys, or German soldiers] with a sword at their backs' to the last minute until an armistice goes into effect.
Allied Supreme Commander
Marshal Ferdinand Foch

I was following the orders of my superior, Marshal Foch, commander in chief of Allied forces in France, issued on 9 November, to keep up the pressure against the retreating enemy until the cease-fire went into effect. Consequently, I not did not order the army to stop fighting, even after the signing of the armistice.
Commander of the American Expeditionary Force
John J Pershing

On the morning of the 11th, commander of the 32nd Infantry Division, Major General William Haan, received a message from a subordinate commanding 63 Brigade asking permission to attack in order to straighten out a dent on his front. Haan slammed back: *I have no intention of throwing away men's lives on the war's last morning to tidy up a map.* The 32nd Infantry Division made no attacks on armistice morning.

18GW988 By contrast to other generals, Major General William Haan, who commanded the 89th Infantry Division, ceased offensive operations when he received news that an armistice had been signed at 5 am and would go into effect at 11 am.

A former operations officer of the 167th Field Artillery Brigade of the 92nd Infantry Division, George K Livermore, gave evidence to a committee set up to investigate the rationale behind some American generals carrying out military operations after the Armistice had been signed at 0500 hrs on the morning of the 11 November 1918, which was to take effect at 11.00. He stated to the committee, in part:

The 92nd Division had been engaged since 5 am on 11 November and had been ordered to launch its final charge at 10:30 am. I lament the little crosses over the graves of the colored lads who died a useless death on that November morning.

He further described the loss of United States Marines killed crossing the Meuse River in the final hours as 'frightful'.

Get into action and get across. I don't expect to see any of you again, but that doesn't matter. You have the honor of a definitive success – give yourself to that.
Major General Summerall

18GW1004 Private Absolum Gunther, 5th Marines, 4 Brigade of Marines, 2nd Infantry Division. He received a gunshot wound during the crossing of the River Meuse on the 10th/11th November. When the cease-fire came into effect after 11 o'clock later that morning they could have simply walked across the two bridges constructed by the engineers, unopposed. Instead, there were 1,100 casualties. One of that number, Private Gunther, was photographed at Red Cross Hospital No.2, Paris. Apart from the entry and exit holes of the bullet there was the added complication of empyema (a condition that causes pus to collect in the body, in this instance, in the lung cavity).

18GW1005 A flimsy construction used by assaulting troops to cross rivers – often under fire – as was the case for the 5th Marines.

18GW1006 A pontoon over the Meuse: the 5th Marine Regiment was to make the assault A witness reported: *At 4 am on the final day of the war the marines emerged from woods and reached the first pontoon bridge. There was a mist obscuring the far bank and as the men crowded onto the planks the pontoons began to sink below the water sloshing about the men's ankles. The engineers shouted to them to space themselves out. Machine gun bullets began knocking men off. By 4.30 am the marines and infantrymen of the 89th Division had taken Pouilly on the east bank. Their orders were to press on and storm the heights above the town. A runner from General Sumerall's HQ arrived with a message: 'Armistice signed and takes effect at 11:00 o'clock this morning.' Nothing was said about halting the fighting in the meantime.*

18GW1008 How men of the 64th Infantry Regiment, 7th Infantry Division received news of the Armistice, Min de Jaulny, 11 November 1918. During its thirty-three days on the front line, the 7th Division suffered 1,709 casualties, including 204 killed in action and 1,505 wounded in action.

18GW996 Among many American artillery batteries, gun crews sought to fire off a final round – a parting shot to signal the end of the great war. At 10.59 hrs 'Calamity Jane', 11th Field Artillery, positioned at the Bois de la Haie on the Laneuville-sur-Meuse – Beauclair road. fired its final hostile round.

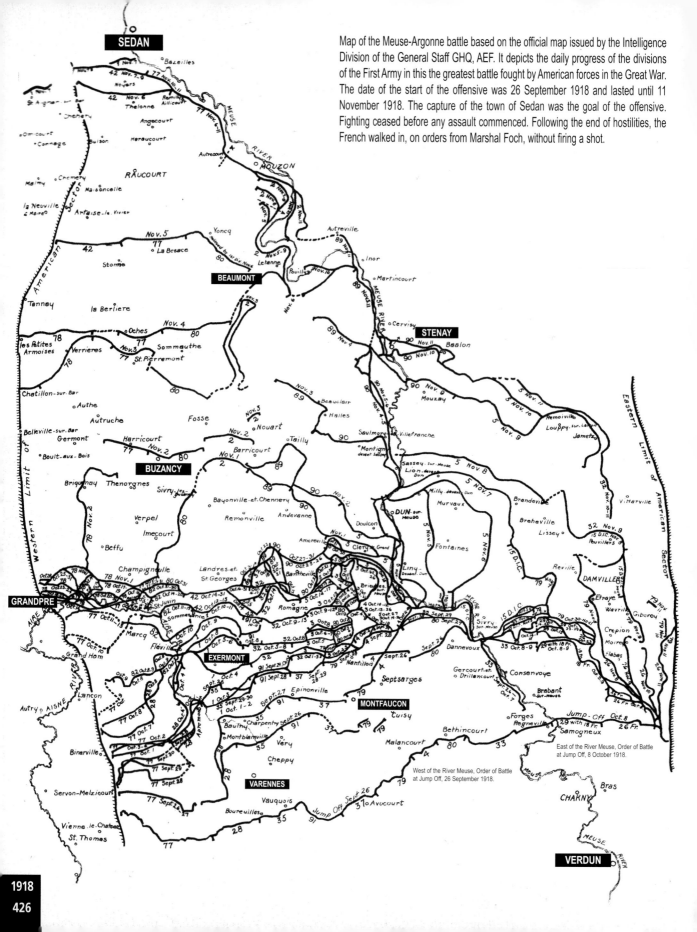

Map of the Meuse-Argonne battle based on the official map issued by the Intelligence Division of the General Staff GHQ, AEF. It depicts the daily progress of the divisions of the First Army in this the greatest battle fought by American forces in the Great War. The date of the start of the offensive was 26 September 1918 and lasted until 11 November 1918. The capture of the town of Sedan was the goal of the offensive. Fighting ceased before any assault commenced. Following the end of hostilities, the French walked in, on orders from Marshal Foch, without firing a shot.

18GW1023 African American officers of 366th Infantry on the *Aquitania*. Left to right: Lieutenant C L Abbot, South Dakota; Captain Joseph L Lowe, Pacific Grove, California; Lieutenant A R Fisher, Lyles, Indiana, winner of Distinguished Service Cross; Captain E White, Pine Bluff, Arkansas.

18GW768 Some of the African American soldiers of the 369th Infantry Regiment (15th New York) who won the Croix de Guerre for gallantry in action. Left to right. Front row: Private Ed Williams, Herbert Taylor, Private Leon Fraitor, Private Ralph Hawkins. Back Row: Sergeant H. D. Prinas, Sergeant. Dan Strorms, Private Joe Williams, Private Alfred Hanley, and Corporal T. W. Taylor. Their courage was especially noteworthy, as they had to face a determined enemy and mindless, prejudiced commanders and men on their own side.

18GW1009 At 11 am precisely this gun section of Battery D, 105th Field Artillery, fired their last shell of the of the war, then hoisted the Stars and Stripes and cheered for the Signal Corps Cameraman.

Chapter Seven:
Battle of Amiens – The Hindenburg Line – Advance to Victory

18GW1025 Americans with Australians at the Battle of Hamel. A forward post 4th July 1918. The Americans may be identified by their erect collars. The presence of American troops in the conflict was beginning to make a marked difference.

18GW1026 A German artilleryman caught in a shell blast along with several draft horses. Some eight million horses died during the four years of war. Life had become very cheap during the four years' conflict.

18GW1037 Field Marshal Sir Douglas Haig inspecting some of Sir Arthur Currie's Canadians, August 1918.

The **Battle of Amiens** was the opening phase of the Allied offensive which began on 8 August 1918 and that ultimately led to the end of the Great War. The British Fourth Army, commanded by Sir Henry Rawlinson, played the decisive role. The Amien battle had a significant effect on German morale and large numbers began surrending from the outset. Erich Ludendorff, effectively commander of the German armies, described the first day of the battle as *der Schwarzer Tag des deutschen Heeres* (the black day of the German Army). Amiens was one of the first major battles involving armoured warfare and marked the end of trench warfare on the Western Front; fighting becoming mobile once again until the armistice was signed on 11 November 1918.

The battle began at 4.20 am with Rawlinson's Fourth Army: the British III Corps attacked north of the Somme; the Australian Corps to the south of the river; the Canadian Corps on the right flank of the Australians. The French First Army, under General Debeney, south of the Australians, began its advance supported, by a battalion of seventy-two Whippet tanks. On the second day the Germans began withdrawing. The Allies had captured nearly 50,000 prisoners and 500 guns by 27 August. Tanks had penetrated twelve miles into German positions by 13 August 1918. Field Marshal Haig refused the request of Marshal Foch to continue the offensive, preferring instead to launch a fresh offensive by Byng's Third Army between the Ancre and Scarpe rivers.

BRITISH FOURTH ARMY

British III Corps	Australian Corps	Canadian Corps	Cavalry Corps

Sir Richard Butler	John Monash	Sir Arthur Currie	Sir Charles Kavanagh

British III Corps
47th (London) Division
12th (Eastern) Division
18th (Eastern) Division
58th (London) Division
10th Tank Battalion:
  36 Mark V tanks

ARMY RESERVE
17th (Northern) Division
32nd Division
63rd (Royal Naval) Division
9th Tank Battalion: 36 Mark V tanks

Australian Corps
1st Australian Division
2nd Australian Division
3rd Australian Division
4th Australian Division
5th Australian Division
33rd US Division
5th Tank Brigade:
2nd, 8th, 13th Bn Tank Corps with 108 Mark V tanks; 15th Bn Tank Corps with 36 Mark V tanks; 17th (Armoured Car) Bn

Canadian Corps
1st Canadian Division
2nd Canadian Division
3rd Canadian Division
4th Canadian Division
4th Tank Brigade:
108 Mark V tanks, 36 Mark V tanks

Cavalry Corps
1st Cavalry Division
2nd Cavalry Division
3rd Cavalry Division
3rd Tank Brigade: 72 Whippet tanks of **3 Bn** and **6 Bn Tank Corps**

Royal Air Force
Major General Salmond

V Brigade
15th (Corps) Wing – 110 aircraft
22nd (Army) Wing – 222 aircraft
IX Brigade
9th Wing – 2 fighter sqns, 2 bomber sqns, 1 reconnaissance sqn. (99 aircraft)
51st Wing – 3 fighter sqns, 2 bomber sqns. (101 aircraft)
54th Wing – 2 night-fighter sqns, 4 night-bomber sqns (76 aircraft)
III Brigade (available in support)
13th (Army) Wing – 136 aircraft
I Brigade (available in support) – 19 aircraft
X Brigade (available in support) – 19 aircraft

Map labels (cities and features)
Roermond, ANTWERP, Ostend, Bruges, Ecloo, Nieuport, Thourout, Ghent, Schelde, Demer, Termonde, Dunkirk, Dixmude, Roulers, Louvain, Maastricht, Aachen (Aix la Chapelle), Calais, Ypres, Isegham, Oudenarde, BRUSSELS, St.Omer, Courtrai, LIÉGE, Roubaix, Ath, Soignies, Namur, Meuse, GERMAN O.H.L., Spa, LILLE, Tournai, Mons, Lens, St. Amand, Condé, Binche, Charleroi, Douai, Valenciennes, Sambre, Beaumont, Arras, Cambrai, Aulnoy, Givet, Bapaume, Le Cateau, Landrecies, Chimay, Péronne, La Capelle, Oise, Somme, Amiens, Guise, Hirson, St.Quentin, Liart, Sedan, Roye, Ham, Donchery, Montdidier, Noyon, La Fère, Mauzon, Stenay, Laon, Rethel, Longuyon, Armistice signed here, Rethondes, Craonne, Aisne, Buzancy, Azannes, Oise, Soissons, Grandpré, Dun, Briey, RHEIMS, Verdun, Conflans, METZ, Pagny, Pont-à-Mousson, BELGIUM, HOLLAND, KAISER, GERMANY, Moselle

Henry Rawlinson
BRITISH FOURTH ARMY

Eugène Debeney
FRENCH FIRST ARMY

Louis Humbert
FRENCH THIRD ARMY

von der Marwitz
SECOND ARMY

Erich Ludendorff
GENERAL STAFF

von Hutier
EIGHTEENTH ARMY

0 — 50
Miles

——— Allied front line on 8 August 1918
– – – Allied front line on 11 November 1918
▢ Ground gained by Allies

Success of the Allied offensive during the Battle of Amiens began what became known as the **Hundred Days Offensive** (from 8 August to 11 November 1918), leading to the defeat of the Central Powers on the Western Front. The offensive pushed the Germans almost out of France, forcing them to retreat beyond the Hindenburg Line and up to their borders and was followed by an armistice. However, large areas of Belgium were still occupied when the surrender occured.

18GW1027 The British offensive in front of Amien began on 8 August 1918. The picture shows the 102nd Howitzer Battery, 2nd Artillery Brigade, 1st Australian Division, brought from Flanders for the battle. The opening of the offensive was not preceded by a fierce bombardment that had heralded other attacks, as secrecy was the ploy. Tanks did the work of heavy guns destroying enemy strongpoints and the field guns and howitzers came into operation, following up the infantry with sustained bombardment.

18GW1034 An officer, Lieutenant Rupert Downes MC, B Company, 29th Battalion, 5th Australian Division, addressing his platoon before the advance upon the second objective, 8 am, 8 August 1918. They are near the double village of Warfusée-Lamotte. Despite its diminutive size, the platoon seen here has three Lewis guns, an indication of the increased employment of light machine guns used by the British in the last months of the war. There was a heavy morning mist which mingled with smoke laid down by the artillery to cover the first phase and it is still evident in this photograph.

18GW1044 Artillery in support of 8 Australian Brigade near Warfusée-Lamotte, 8 am, 8 August 1918. The first objective had already been attained and the artillery, according to plan, has followed up to support the second advance.

18GW1045 Mark V tanks advancing in the second phase of the attack. Around 340 fighting tanks led the way, backed by 120 supply tanks. Along with this armoured drive were 72 Whippet tanks working with the cavalry.

18GW1049 German prisoners just captured hurrying past 'Susan Wood', concerned at the shells from their own artillery north of the River Somme, which could see them as they topped the hill.

18GW1048 Six German officers marching at the head of their men captured at Accroche Wood. These officers said that the attack came as a complete surprise and was well planned.

18GW1050 German prisoners being marched into the city of Amiens. On the first day of the battle the British Fourth Army took 13,000 prisoners, while the French captured a further 3,000.

18GW1047 A group of seven German prisoners carrying a wounded comrade in a blanket along the Amiens-Roye road near Beaucourt, 9 August. The moment of surrender is especially dangerous as the captors, with their blood up and in a high state of nervous tension, may shoot them out of hand. The camera has caught the emotional strain evident on their faces. Note the contrasting ages of these prisoners: young boys and elderly veterans. The Germans were running short of reserves in manpower and the morale of their soldiers was at a low ebb. The British and French attack in the Amiens sector of the line had come as a complete surprise as secrecy of the build-up for the offensive had been successfully maintained. In addition, there had been no preliminary artillery bombardment to soften up the defences

18GW1051, 18GW1052. The German High Command knew that the war was all but lost from 8 August 1918, with the resounding success of the Allied Amiens offensive. German prisoners are passing Allied anti-aircraft guns near Mericourt-l'Abbé, on the first day of the Battle of Amiens. Prisoners resting at the roadside could only look on as their comrades, recently captured, arrive to add to their numbers.

18GW1046, 18GW1053. A Canadian 60-pounder battery in action 10 August. They are setting fuses on shells and placing them ready for firing and loading them into the breech.

18GW1054 Slamming a shell into the breech of an 18-pounder, this Australian gun crew works fast to support the advancing infantry. The Canadian and Australian Corps were at the forefront of the British advance and their attached artillery proved highly effective.

18GW1055 Tanks advancing for the third phase: a detachment of the 15th Tank Brigade passing through the infantry towards the third objective (six miles from their starting point). The longer tanks, 'Mark V Star', were each to carry twenty-four infantrymen; however, the heat, fumes and noise inside caused the infantry to march along outside.

18GW1057 A 9.2 inch howitzer of the 95th Siege Battalion, Royal Garrison Artillery, laying down fire in support of the infantry during the Battle of Amiens.

18GW1056 Canadian infantry resting in a huge shell crater during the Amiens battle.

18GW1059 An enlarged Mark V female tank (armed with machine guns instead of a 6-pounder cannon, was called a male) in the streets of Méaulte, 22 August 1918.

18GW1058, 18GW1060. Tanks on a country road with prisoners heading back towards the city of Amiens. One wounded British Tommy is being helped along by a German prisoner. Once they had stopped trying to kill each other, all further animosity seemed pointless.

18GW1061 Plainly marked supply tanks supporting the fighting tanks by carrying fuel and ammunition.

18GW1069 Austin armoured cars in use by the Australians, although the lead vehicle is flying the French tricolour and may have been acting as a lead scout car.

18GW1064 A Canadian Autocar armed with three Vickers machine guns, one fixed firing forward and two mounted openly. With open warfare being waged, in contrast to trench fighting, armoured cars and cavalry were employed effectively for the first time since 1914 and the opening phases of the Great War.

18GW1070 A wrecked Canadian armoured car with one of the crew lying dead. Note that the dead soldier's boots appear to have been taken.

18GW1063,18GW1068. A German gun battery positioned on along the edge of a wood has been abandoned and the position occupied by Canadian infantry.

18GW1074 Canadians in a captured German howitzer battery position. The 21 cm Mörser could fire a shell 10,280 yards and a good crew could load two shells every minute.

18GW1072 Australians among the old Somme trench system near Crépey Wood (on the skyline) during the attack upon the ruined village of Lihons by the Australian 10th Battalion. One of the German guns which destroyed tanks operating with 2 Brigade, 9 August, is in the photograph.

18GW1073 Canadians advancing on the village of Lihons, with a tank attacking a German machine gun position which was on the north side of the railway line embankment. The men in the photograph were under fire.

18GW1071 Commander of the British Fourth Army's Canadian Corps, Lieutenant General Sir Arthur Currie, visiting a park for captured German artillery pieces. (Currie's nickname was 'Guts and Gaiters' – is that what his men are thinking in this photograph?)

18GW1075 Canadians clearing out surrendering Germans from dugouts during the Amiens offensive.

1918

448

18GW1076, 18GW1077, 18GW1078. Prisoners taken by the Canadians: both guards and prisoners are putting on gas masks in one of these photographs at this aid post as gas shells are exploding in the vicinity.

18GW1118 Australians passing captured German trenches in the advance at Lamotte-Warfusée, 8 August 1918

18GW1081 Field Marshal Sir Douglas Haig seen here at Domart during a visit to the Fourth Army, 11 August. The men are Canadians of the 85th Canadian Battalion (Nova Scotia Highlanders) and Haig is congratulating them for their part in the Battle of Amiens.

18GW1081 An interesting study in expressions on the faces of these German prisoners captured during the surprise assault carried out by the Fourth Army. Note some of these men have head wounds; Undoubtedly, men seen here would be involved in the second round of hostilities twenty-one years hence as soldiers of Hitler's Third Reich.

18GW1085 Britiah cavalry concentrated near Harbonnières – the cavalry followed through on the success of the infantry but suffered heavy casualties. A horse and rider make for an easy target in modern warfare. However, they remained the most mobile force available even in 1918.

18GW1083 A detachment of the 13th Regiment, Australian Light Horse trotting past Gressaire Wood, 22 August, day of the attack by the Australian 3rd infantry Division and the British divisions north of the Somme at Bray. The second main British attack was officially known as the Battle of Albert. The 13th Regiment would shortly be operating in open country during the advance of the Australian Corps in September.

18GW1088 Reinforcements of the Australian 3 Brigade advancing near Chuignolles on 23 August, about an hour after the first attack south of the Somme (generally known to the Australian rank and file as the 'Battle of Proyart').

18GW1084, 18GW1086. Pioneers of the 3rd Australian Division tackled a bridge over the River Somme Canal at Chipilly which had been blown by the Germans in their retreat. The Germans in breaking down two bridges at this point failed to realise that the longer of the two could be repositioned on the two piers. It was done in just six days by the 3rd Pioneer Battalion.

18GW1087 A Canadian soldier hands out cigarettes to his French allies, men of the French First Army, near Roye, 12 August.

18GW1089 French infantry taking a rest period near an overturned thirty tons German A7V *Sturmpanzerwagen*. Throughout August the French offensive drive had been sluggish, with the exception of the French Tenth Army. The Germans were still on their soil and that of Belgium and they had seen so many efforts to thrown them back to the border falter.

18GW1161 Weapons taken by the French from retreating German formations, seen here in Villers-Cotterets in August 1918.

18GW1162 British entering the ruins of Albert, August 1918. German snipers would need rooting out.

18GW1163, 18GW1164, 18GW1165, 18GW1166. The camera follows this British patrol and captures the action as they engage in a dangerous game of 'cat and mouse': two men scramble up the rubble; a soldier with a telescopic-sighted rifle scans the ruins ahead; an officer also sights up on a suspect building; two Tommies drag a wounded comrade into shelter, taking care not to show themselves.

18GW1090 Aerial view of the devastated town of Albert. In 1916 thousands of British soldiers who fought at the Battle of the Somme passed through Albert, which was situated two miles from the front lines. On top of the Basilica of Notre-Dame de Brebières was the statue of Mary and the infant Jesus, which was knocked askew by a shell in January 1915; superstitious ideas concerning its fall were entertained by French, British and German soldiers. It was destroyed by a British shell when the Germans took the town in April 1918.

18GW1091 The ruined Basilica of Notre-Dame de Brebières in 1918. Written in ink on the back is the following:
The awful destruction of Albert Cathedral [Basilica] mostly during the 1918 fighting. I saw this Cathedral with the famous Virgin still suspended 27 October 1917.

18GW1092 Written in ink on the back of the destroyed railway lines photograph is the following:
Albert, the remains of the railway station after 1918 fighting when Albert practically became a No Man's Land. I last passed through on 28 October 1917.

18GW1080 The Australian 9 Brigade attacked the village of Bray-sur-Somme during the Battle of Albert, 22 August 1918. Pictured was a particularly dangerous corner with a 'Calvaire' (religious shrine) where a German sniper had been operating. He lies dead, having been located and shot from the flank while taking aim.

18GW1093 Original caption reads: *A view of a street in Albert just as the Germans had been pushed out, 23 August 1918.*

18GW1094 Film crew moving towards the action south of Albert. The original caption reads: *Cinema officer going up to film near Méaulte, 23 August 1918.*

18GW1095 An official photograph showing British troops during the Battle of Albert. This picture captures a Platoon advancing by sections, each section led by a non-commissioned officer.

18GW1096 Men of the British 5th Infantry Division on the Miraumont-Bapaume road, near the village of Irles, 21 August 1918.

18GW1099 Men of the British 5th Infantry Division resting and feeding horses near the village of Irles, 21 August 1918.

18GW1101 Sudden raucous laughter and cheering from this gun crew startles the sergeant's mount. Morale was very high as the success of the Amiens battle became increasingly obvious to the Allied soldiers and as trench warfare gave way to open country pursuit of a withdrawing enemy. The gun is a 6-inch howitzer.

18GW1098 The first self-propelled gun, the Gun Carrier Mk I. Forty-eight were made by Kitson and Company, Leeds. The gun was a 60-pounder (or 6-inch howitzer). This one is photographed near the village of Irles in the last week of August 1918.

18GW1097 Tommies check out an abandoned German artillery position during the Battle of Albert, late August 1918.

18GW1102 Men of the Lincolnshire Regiment in a former German trench, September 1918.

18GW1098 A British Lewis gun team following up the German withdrawal.

18GW1103 In the fighting around Proyart this 14-inch naval gun was discovered by the 3rd Australian Infantry Battalion on the edge of Arcy Wood, 23 August 1918. The weapon had been destroyed by the Germans.

18GW1116 French Renault FT tanks and infantry advancing. The FT was the most inovative design launched during the war, it was revolutionary, featuring many characteristics still in use on modern tanks to this day. The FT was also the most produced tank of the war.

18GW1105 This photograph shows the types of British troops engaged in the offensive: scene at a Y.M.C.A. refreshment centre at Corbie, 25 August 1918, showing English, Scottish, Australian and Canadians on their way to or from the front. The original caption comments: *The types of these men are in marked contrast to those of the majority of Germans encountered in this last stage of the war and give some indication of one cause of Allied victory.*

18GW1104 A Section of the 9th Australian Infantry Battalion on patrol and seen here searching German dugouts on the south side of the Somme, half a mile in advance of the front line 25 August 1918.

18GW1115 Canadians celebrating the highly successful breakthrough in the Battle of Amiens. They have obligingly climbed on the tanks at the bidding of the cameraman.

MONT ST QUENTIN AND THE TOWN OF PÉRONNE. From dawn on Saturday, 31 August 1918, until the evening of 3 September, three divisions of the Australian Corps attacked successfully Mont St Quentin and the town of Péronne. At the fighting's conclusion the Australians had secured the high ground overlooking the large town of Péronne. A wide breach had been driven into the German line of defence that the enemy had established on the series of heights lying to the east of the Somme and of the Canal du Nord.

The capture of Mont St. Quentin by the Second Division is a feat of arms worthy of the highest praise. The natural strength of the position is immense, and the tactical value of it, in reference to Péronne and the whole system of the Somme defences, cannot be over-estimated. I am filled with admiration at the gallantry and surpassing daring of the Second Division in winning this important fortress, and I congratulate them with all my heart.
General Rawlinson

18GW1120 General Sir Henry Rawlinson, commander, Fourth British Army, in his advanced headquarters railway carriage, near Péronne, France, 1918.

Lt General Sir John Monash
AUSTRALIAN CORPS

Max von Boehn
ARMY GROUP BOEHN

18GW1122 Mont St Quentin, held by the Germans as part of their line of defence before the Hindenburg Line. Men of the 2nd Australian Division would attack across this ground to fight for the strongpoint.

18GW1107 Infantry of the 24th Battalion awaiting the lifting of the artillery barrage. This photograph was taken minutes before they moved out of the trench to renew the assault on the position known as the Crater, on top of the hill. The 21st, 23rd and 24th Battalions were successful.

18GW1106 Bombardment of Mont St Quentin 0n 1 September 1918. The photograph was taken from Elsa Trench at the time of 6 Brigade's renewed attack on the summit.

18GW1124 Members of the 24th Battalion in a trench, awaiting the lifting of the artillery barrage before the renewed attack that led to the capture of Mont St Quentin.

18GW1125 Men of the 6th Australian Infantry Brigade moving along a communication trench in the renewed assault upon Mont St Quentin.

18GW1134 German dead in a sunken road, a former artillery position.

Sergeant Alby Lowerson VC, 21st Battalion, citation:
For most conspicuous bravery and tactical skill on the 1st September, 1918, during the attack on Mt. St. Quentin, north of Péronne, when very strong opposition was met with early in the attack, and every foot of ground was stubbornly contested by the enemy. Regardless of heavy enemy machine gun fire, Sergeant Lowerson moved about fearlessly directing his men, encouraging them to still greater effort, and finally led them on to the objective. On reaching the objective he saw that the left attacking party was held up by an enemy strong post heavily manned with twelve machine guns. Under the heaviest sniping and machine gun fire, Sergeant Lowerson rallied seven men as a storming party, and directing them to attack the flanks of the post, rushed the strong point, and, by effective bombing, captured it, together with twelve machine guns and thirty prisoners. Though severely wounded in the right thigh, he refused to leave the front line until the prisoners had been disposed of, and the organization and consolidation of the post had been thoroughly completed. Throughout a week of operations, his leadership and example had a continual influence on the men serving under him, whilst his prompt and effective action at a critical juncture allowed the forward movement to be carried on without delay, thus ensuring the success of the attack.
—*The London Gazette*, December 1918

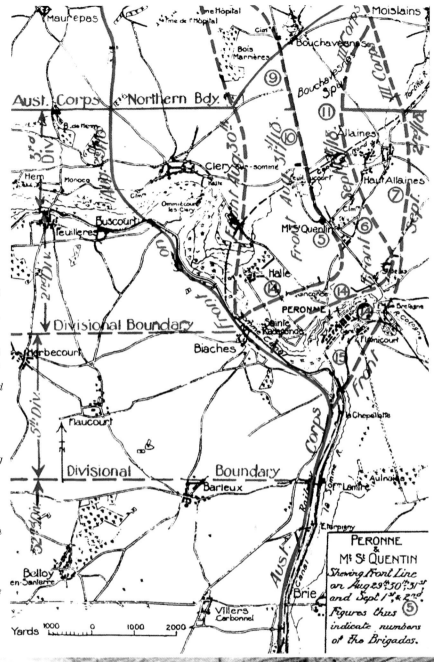

18GW1125, 18GW1126. The first wave of A Company, 21st Australian Infantry Battalion, having advanced from Elsa Trench, reach a high brick wall surrounding the wood at Mont St Quentin and are seen to approach the gaps with caution. Corporal Phillip Starr later wrote: *When we neared the village we were for a time concealed, and were enabled to take up our position close by a brick wall which seemed to run along the lower edge of the village. From here we started on the actual attack.'*

18GW1132 Late on the afternoon of 1 September 1918 A Company had reached a German trench to the south-east of Mont St Quentin in the countryside to the left of the road which today runs into Péronne. They dug in and waited for the inevitable German counter-attacks. The summit of Mont St Quentin was now firmly in Australian hands.

18GW1109 Captain Sullivan, 21st Australian Infantry Battalion, leads his men along a bullet-swept road at Mont St Quentin, 1 September 1918. Captain Sullivan was later killed on the 5 October 1918 in the AIF's last action of the war.

18GW1135 Scene of attack on Péronne, 1 September 1918; the 53rd Battalion crossed this area but was halted by fire from the ramparts (on the right). The 54th Battalion, however, had crossed the town moat and seized half the town.

Private Robert Mactier VC, 23rd Battalion, posthumously awarded the Victoria Cross, citation:
For most conspicuous bravery and devotion to duty on the morning of the 1st September, 1918, during the attack on the village of Mt. St. Quentin. Prior to the advance of the battalion, it was necessary to clear up several enemy strong points close to our line. This the bombing patrols sent forward failed to effect, and the battalion was unable to move. Private Mactier, single handed, and in daylight, thereupon jumped out of the trench, rushed past the block, closed with and killed the machine gun garrison of eight men with his revolver and bombs, and threw the enemy machine gun over the parapet. Then, rushing forward about 20 yards, he jumped into another strong point held by a garrison of six men, who immediately surrendered. Continuing to the next block through the trench, he disposed of an enemy machine gun which had been enfilading our flank advancing troops, and was then killed by another machine gun at close range. It was entirely due to this exceptional valour and determination of Private Mactier that the battalion was able to move on to its 'jumping off' trench and carry out the successful operation of capturing the village of Mont St. Quentin a few hours later.
—*The London Gazette*, 13 December 1918

18GW1110 In front of Anvil Wood, looking back through a gap in the German barbed wire through which part of the 53rd Battalion (New South Wales) advanced towards Péronne, 1 September. A German machine gun trained on this gap caused many casualties. In the background, to the left of the wood, a shell can be seen exploding on a British Main Dressing Station.

Lieutenant Edgar Thomas Towner VC, 2nd Battalion, Machine Gun Corps, citation:

For most conspicuous bravery, initiative and devotion to duty on 1st September, 1918, in the attack on Mont St. Quentin, near Péronne, when in charge of four Vickers guns. During the early stages of the advance he located and captured, single-handed, an enemy machine-gun which was causing casualties, and by turning it on the enemy inflicted severe losses. Subsequently, by the skilful, tactical handling of his guns, he cut off and captured twenty-five of the enemy. Later, by fearless reconnaissance under heavy fire, and by the energy, foresight and promptitude with which he brought fire to bear on various enemy groups, he gave valuable support to the infantry advance. Again, when short of ammunition, he secured an enemy machine-gun, which he mounted and fired in full view of the enemy, causing the enemy to retire further, and enabling our infantry to advance. Under intense fire, although wounded, he maintained the fire of this gun at a very critical period. During the following night he steadied and gave valuable support to a small detached post, and by his coolness and cheerfulness inspirited the men in a great degree. Throughout the night he kept close watch by personal reconnaissance on the enemy movements, and was evacuated exhausted thirty hours after being wounded. The valour and resourcefulness of Lieutenant Towner undoubtedly saved a very critical situation, and contributed largely to the success of the attack.

—***The London Gazette***, 14 December 1918

18GW1127 Australian sretcher bearers of 6 Brigade bringing in an injured soldier to a Dressing Station.

18GW1133 A German machine gun position on the ramparts of the town of Péronne with a clear view towards Anvil Wood and the barbed wire, through which Australian soldiers attacked Péronne on 1 September 1918.

18GW1066 A German machine gun team waiting for the Tommies to crest the hill. Right to the very end of the war German machine gun operators proved to be effective and continued to cause casualties. The German army withdrawal towards their own national borders was no rout.

18GW1148 A machine gun position established by the Australian 54th Battalion during its attack on German forces in the ruins of Péronne, 1 September 1918.

18GW1139 The 53rd Battalion entered Péronne at this point early on the morning of 2 September 1918.

Alexander Buckley posthumous VC, citation:

For most conspicuous bravery and self-sacrifice at Peronne during the operations on the 1 and 2 September, 1918. After passing the first objective his half company and part of the company on the flank were held up by a machine gun nest. With one man he rushed the post shooting four of the occupants and taking twenty-two prisoners. Later, on reaching a moat, it was found that another machine gun nest commanded the only available footbridge. Whilst this was being engaged from a flank Corporal Buckley endeavoured to cross the bridge and rush the post, but was killed in the attempt. Throughout the advance he had displayed great initiative, resource and courage, and by his efforts to save his comrades from casualties, he set a fine example of self-sacrificing devotion to duty.

—**The London Gazette**, 14 December 1918

William Currey VC, citation:

When the battalion was suffering heavy casualties from a 77 mm. field gun at very close range, Private Currey, without hesitation, rushed forward under intense machine-gun fire and succeeded in capturing the gun single-handed after killing the entire crew. Later, when the advance of the left flank was checked by an enemy strong point, Private Currey crept around the flank and engaged the post with a Lewis gun. Finally, he rushed the post single-handed, causing many casualties. Subsequently he volunteered to carry orders for the withdrawal of an isolated company, and this he succeeded in doing despite shell and rifle fire, returning later with valuable information. Throughout the operations his striking example of coolness, determination, and utter disregard of danger had a most inspiring effect on his comrades, and his gallant work contributed largely to the success of the operations.

18GW1131 Australian troops and tanks in the streets of Péronne shortly after its capture and occupation. The town would become a firm base for continued operations.

Arthur Charles Hall VC citation:

For most conspicuous bravery, brilliant leadership and devotion to duty at Peronne on the 1 and 2 September, 1918. During the attack on the 1 September a machine-gun post was checking the advance. Single-handed, he rushed the position, shot four of the occupants and captured nine others and two machine guns. Then crossing the objective with a small party, Corporal Hall afforded excellent covering support to the remainder of the company. Continuously in advance of the main party, he located enemy posts of resistance and personally led parties to the assault. In this way he captured many small parties of prisoners and machine guns. On the morning of 2 September, during a heavy barrage, he carried to safety a comrade who had been dangerously wounded and was urgently in need of medical attention, and immediately returned to his post. The energy and personal courage of this gallant non-commissioned officer contributed largely to the success of the operations, throughout which he showed utter disregard of danger and inspired confidence in all.

18GW1140 Ordnance stores of the Australian Corps in Péronne cavalry barracks.

18GW1141 Clothing store of the Australian Ordnance Corps, Péronne barracks.

18GW1142 Armourers' workshops of the Australian Ordnance Corps in Péronne barracks.

18GW1140 A file of the Australian 56th Battalion in the process of transfer to the northern side of the Somme near Clery-sur-Somme.

On 29 September 1918, the strongly defended Hindenburg Line was attacked over a four mile wide land bridge between Bellicourt and Vendhuille, where the St Quentin Canal ran underground through a tunnel. After eight weeks of continuous action Australian battalions were down to only 300 men available for action. The Australians were reinforced by inexperienced American troops with a unit strength three times that of the exhausted Australians. In three days of hard fighting, with Lewis guns and grenades, the Australians captured the first two German lines which had been the American objectives. On 3 October 1918, Australian troops broke through the last defensive system of the Hindenburg Line, the third (Beaurevoir) line. Two days later, they captured Montbrehain village. These were the final infantry actions fought by Australian soldiers on the Western Front. The five Australian divisions were withdrawn for a rest and were heading up the line into battle again on 11 November 1918, the day the Armistice was declared.

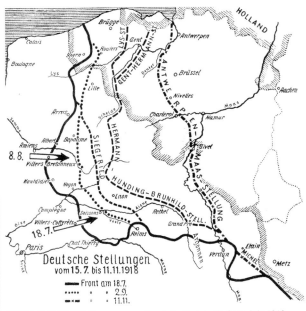

18GW1144, 18GW1145. German map showing withdrawals from July 1918 to 11 November. A section of the German main defence, the Hindenburg Line, a huge mass of barbed wire, October, 1918.

18GW1065 Australians approaching the Hindenburg Line.

18GW1154, 18GW1151. Attack on the Hindenburg Line, British Mk V tanks carrying 'cribs' to help crossing the trenches, and troops going forward near Bellicourt, 29 September 1918. Note the German prisoners mingled with the Tommies.

18GW1149 Troops of the Royal Inniskilling Fusiliers, 36th (Ulster) Division, advancing from Ravelsburg Ridge to the outskirts of Neuve Eglise, 1 September 1918.

18GW1150 Battle of St. Quentin Canal. Wire in front of the Hindenburg Line, near Bellicourt, 4 October 1918.

18GW1157 British troops crossing a section of the St Quentin Canal after breaking the Hindenburg Line defences 2 October 1918.

18GW1152 The St Quentin Canal was bridged by the Royal Engineers following its capture.

18GW1155 The Sambre–Oise Canal saw Lock No 1 on the Sambre canal where the 2nd Battalion Royal Sussex Regiment crossed, supported by Royal Engineers. One of the last Allied successes before the Armistice.

The famous war poet, Wilfred Owen, was killed in action during the crossing of the Sambre–Oise Canal, (exactly one week before the signing of the Armistice that ended the war) Monday, November 4. At 5.45am, an attempt was made to cross the canal. Owen and his party came under heavy machine-gun fire from Germans on the opposite bank. While helping his men to get planks across, Owen was hit and killed.

18GW1156 The St Quentin Canal passes under the village of Bellicourt in a tunnel three miles long. The Hindenburg Line ran west of the village and the barges in the tunnel were used to shelter German troops. Three miles south of Bellicourt is the village of Bellenglise. The 46th (North Midland) Division stormed the Hindenburg Line at Bellenglise and captured 4,000 prisoners and seventy guns. The 30th American Infantry Division captured Bellicourt and Nauroy, which were then cleared by the 5th Australian Division.

18GW1147 Brigadier General J V Campbell VC, addressing troops of 137 Brigade, 46 (North Midland) Division, from the Riqueval Bridge over the St Quentin Canal after breaking the Hindenburg Line defences 2 October 1918.

18GW1172 The King and Queen of the Belgians, Albert and Elisabeth, saluting the flag, in the square at Bruges, 25 October 1918, celebrate the town's freedom.

18GW1167, 18GW1168. Bringing up suuplies to the advancing Allies with ammunition mules and artillery gun carriages.

18GW1169 Commander of the British Second Army, General Plumer, held up by traffic on the lines of advance.

18GW1170 German prisoners help stretcher wounded into a sunken road recently captured by the Canadians. Canadian support transport throngs the road.

18GW1171 German prisoners carrying wounded to an Advanced Dressing Station after a fight with the Australians.

18GW1175, 18GW1176. Crossing the Scheldt under fire; a Lewis gun team in the ruins. The city of Valenciennes was captured by the British on the morning of 2 November 1918. Canadian troops under General Currie encountered strong opposition as they approached the outskirts but, after a hard struggle, they crushed all resistance and entered the city.

18GW1177 Happy citzens of Valenciennes given a lift back to their homes after the retreating Germans had flooded the streets.

18GW1159 German infantry, disconsolate and beaten, resting during the general withdrawal from occupied France and Belgium to their own frontiers.

18GW1146 The Prince of Wales, with General Currie and General Watson, on a street in Denain, France, shortly after its capture by the Canadian troops. Denain is near the border of Belgium and the French town of Valenciennes, which was taken on 4 November, 1918.

18GW1173 Germans withdrawing through the streets of Brussels heading back the way they came four years ago to their own borders. Already flags of the Allies decorate the buildings.

MAUBEUGE

PORTE DE MONS

18GW1158 Irish Guards at the Mons Gate of Maubeuge, which had been held by the Germans for fifty months. The British army was back where it first engaged the enemy at Mons in August 1914 (See volume One). British troops entered Maubeuge 9 November; it shared with Mons the distinction of being one of the places avenged in the closing hours of the war. It was recaptured by the Guards Division and the 62nd Division, when men of the Grenadiers broke through the German rear guard.

18GW1160 Marching through Mons to the music of the pipes. Canadian troops had been the ones to march into Mons to relieve it. Typical scene on the streets of Mons as crowds flocked out to hail with delight the men who had freed them. The invaders were gone on the 11 November, the very day when the Germans had submitted to the harsh terms of the armistice dictated by the Allies.

CROIX PLACE

18GW1178, 18GW1180, 18GW1181. A German delegation in five cars bearing white flags arrived in the French lines on the 7 November and was escorted across a war devastated landscape to where a railway train awaited them. They were then taken aboard Ferdinand Foch's private train, parked in a railway siding in the forest of Compiègne. The Germans were handed a list of Allied demands and given seventy-two hours to agree. There was no question of negotiation and the Germans could only protest at the harshness of the terms. On Sunday 10 November, they were shown newspapers from Paris informing them that the Kaiser had abdicated. That same day the Germans signed. The Armistice was agreed at 5.00 am on the 11 November 1918, to come into effect at 11 am Paris time (noon German time).

The armistice contained the following main points:

A. Western Front
Termination of hostilities on the Western Front, on land and in the air, within six hours of signature.

Immediate evacuation of France, Belgium, Luxembourg, and Alsace-Lorraine within 15 days. Sick and wounded may be left for Allies to care.

Immediate repatriation of all inhabitants of those four territories in German hands.

Surrender of matériel: 5,000 artillery pieces, 25,000 machine guns, 3,000 minenwerfers, 1,700 aircraft (including all night bombers), 5,000 railway locomotives, 150,000 railcars and 5,000 road trucks.

Evacuation of territory on the west side of the Rhine plus 19 mile radius bridgeheads of the east side of the Rhine at the cities of Mainz, Koblenz, and Cologne within 31 days.

Vacated territory to be occupied by Allied and US troops, maintained at Germany's expense.

No removal or destruction of civilian goods or inhabitants in evacuated territories and all military matériel and premises to be left intact.

All minefields on land and sea to be identified.

All means of communication (roads, railways, canals, bridges, telegraphs, telephones) to be left intact, as well as everything needed for agriculture and industry.

B. Eastern and African Fronts
Immediate withdrawal of all German troops in Romania and in what were the Ottoman Empire, the Austro-Hungarian Empire and the Russian Empire back to German territory as it was on 1 August 1914. The Allies to have access to these countries.

Renunciation of the Treaty of Brest-Litovsk with Russia and of the Treaty of Bucharest with Romania.

Evacuation of German forces in Africa.

C. At sea
Immediate cessation of all hostilities at sea and surrender intact of all German submarines within 14 days.

Listed German surface vessels to be interned within 7 days and the rest disarmed.

Free access to German waters for Allied ships and for those of the Netherlands, Norway, Denmark and Sweden.

The naval blockade of Germany to continue.

Immediate evacuation of all Black Sea ports and handover of all captured Russian vessels.

D. General
Immediate release of all Allied prisoners of war and interned civilians, without reciprocity.

Pending a financial settlement, surrender of assets looted from Belgium, Romania and Russia.

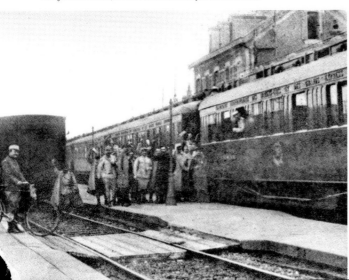

Evening Standard

No. 29,428.   LONDON, MONDAY, NOVEMBER 11, 1918.   ONE PENNY.

END OF THE WAR

GERMANY SIGNS OUR TERMS & FIGHTING STOPPED AT 11 O'CLOCK TO-DAY.

ALLIES TRIUMPHANT.

FOCH AND LLOYD GEORGE TELL NEWS THAT SENT THE WORLD REJOICING.

BRITISH BACK AT MONS!

The following historic announcement, which means that the world war has come to an end at last, was issued by Mr. Lloyd George to the nation at 10.20 this morning:—

"THE ARMISTICE WAS SIGNED AT 5 a.m. THIS MORNING, AND HOSTILITIES ARE TO CEASE ON ALL FRONTS AT 11 a.m. TO-DAY."

The following message was sent out to-day through the wireless stations of the French Government.

"Marshal Foch to Commanders-in-Chief.

"Hostilities will cease on the whole front as from November 11th, at 11 o'clock (French time).

"The Allied troops will not, until a further order, go beyond the line reached on that date and at that hour.

(Signed) MARSHAL FOCH.

The armistice negotiations opened on Friday morning, when the Germans were given until 11 a.m. to-day to accept or reject the Allied terms.

The signing of the terms of course means the end of the war, as the safeguards are such that it will be impossible for Germany to renew the struggle.

FULL ARMISTICE TERMS

EVACUATION TO THE RHINE AND BRIDGEHEADS FOR ALLIES.

U-BOATS TO SURRENDER.

GUNS HANDED OVER AND BATTLE SHIPS DISARMED.

REPATRIATING PRISONERS.

The terms of the armistice signed by the German plenipotentiaries were read in the House of Commons this afternoon by Mr. Lloyd George.

The armistice terms include evacuation of invaded territories, Belgium, France, Alsace-Lorraine, Luxembourg, to be completed within 14 days.

Railways of Alsace-Lorraine to be handed over.

German troops who have not left these territories within 14 days to be treated as prisoners of war. The occupation by the Allied and United States forces will keep pace with the evacuation.

The evacuation by the enemy of Rhine lands must be completed within 16 days.

Immediate repatriation without reciprocity of Allied and United States prisoners.

All German troops in Russia, Rumania, and elsewhere to be withdrawn. Complete abandonment of the treaties of Bukharest and Brest-Litovsk.

Immediate cessation of all hostilities at sea. Handing over to Allies and United States of all submarines.

The surrender by the German Government of the following equipment:— 5000 guns, of which 2500 will be heavy and 2500 field guns, 30,000 machine-guns, and a large number of trench-mortars.

Six battle cruisers, ten battleships, eight light cruisers, 50 destroyers, and other services are to be disarmed, and the Allies reserve the right to occupy Heligoland to enable them to enforce the terms of the armistice.

BREST-LITOVSK TREATY ABANDONED.

By Our Parliamentary Representatives.

HOUSE OF COMMONS, Monday.

There are large crowds in Palace Yard outside the Houses of Parliament. Mr. Lloyd George arrived in a motorcar, accompanied by Mrs. Lloyd George, and Mr. Bonar Law, Sir Eric Geddes following behind in another motorcar. The two cars were preceded by a mounted police-man, who made a way through the cheering crowds.

When the Prime Minister entered the House he was greeted by his colleagues with tumultuous cheering. Immediately at the conclusion of prayers the Prime Minister was called upon by the Speaker.

Mr. Lloyd George said : The armistice, as has already been announced in the Press, was signed this morning at 5 o'clock, after a discussion which was prolonged all night. I will read to the House of Commons the conditions of the armistice, in so far as they have reached me up to the present.

I have to warn the House and the public that we only received such corrections as that were rendered necessary by the new conditions by telephone, and there is a possibility that there may be a few mistakes, but substantially this represents the conditions which Germany has accepted.

CLAUSES RELATING TO THE WESTERN FRONT.

Cessation of hostilities by land and in the air six hours after the signature of the armistice.

AT THE PALACE.

TERRIFIC OVATION FOR THE KING AND QUEEN.

Wonderful scenes of rejoicing were witnessed outside Buckingham Palace. As soon as the news became generally known in the West End thousands of people flocked towards Buckingham Palace, and cheered for a considerable time. Soldiers passing on military motors joined in the glorification, people in khaki stood and waved and the cheering was borne down the Mall. Soldiers passing on military motors joined in the glorification, people in khaki stood and waved and the cheering was borne down the Mall. They had not yet through the second verse when the music stopped, and from one of the open windows emerged the King and Queen, accompanied by Princess Mary and the Duke of Connaught. They faced the multitude from the balcony.

The appearance of the Royal party was greeted with enthusiasm. As the band played the National Anthem the King as usual solemnly, but when the strains of "Rule, Britannia," rang out his Majesty raised his naval cap and waved it enthusiastically. This led to a further demonstration on the part of the crowd.

Three thunderous cheers were given for Lloyd George, and immediately following considerable merriment was caused by the roar of an old woman : "Poor old Tirpitz. We have Smuts." his whiskers."

During the demonstration the Queen frequently waved her handkerchief in expression of her warm sympathy with the joy of the crowd. Addressing the crowd from the balcony of the Palace the vast crowd, the King said :

"With you I rejoice and thank God for the victories which the Allied armies have won and brought hostilities to an end and peace within sight."

When the gates were commanded to see there was renewed cheering and flag-waving, while a party of munition girls formed themselves into a ring and danced and sang in joyous holiday mood.

At 12.30 the massed bands of the Guards assembled in the forecourt, and played the patriotic airs and other bright selections, to the great delight of the tremendous crowd assembled

PEACE IN BRIEF.

BRITISH RECAPTURED MONS BEFORE THE FIGHTING STOPPED!

Armistice signed 5 a.m. to-day.

Hostilities ceased at 11 a.m.

British recaptured Mons this morning, and thus ended the war where our "Old Contemptibles" began it for us.

Erzberger evidently signed the armistice at Foch's G.H.Q. for the Germans.

German armies must evacuate to the east bank of the Rhine in 31 days.

London's lights are to go up to-night (full details on another page).

BACK TO THE RHINE.

One of the armistice terms is the withdrawal of the German armies to the east bank of the Rhine. The following table of distances will be of interest therefore :—

Towns.	Front.	Miles.
Ghent	Belgian	140
Mons	British	148
Maubeuge	British	155
Mezieres	French	162
Stenay	American	150
Alsace	American	20

ENVOYS RETURNING.

The German Plenipotentiaries are returning to Spa to-day.

THE ORDER OF GOING.

Armistices have been signed as follows:

Bulgaria	Sept. 29, 1918
Turkey	Oct. 30, 1918
Austria-Hungary	Nov. 3, 1918

morning, and the war ceased at 11 o'clock this morning.

Immediate evacuation of invaded territories,

(Continued on Page 8.)

Chapter Eight: Some Consequences of this Global War

18GW1182 The poor of Berlin rummaging in refuse heaps for scraps of food. Some claim 750,000 German civilians died from starvation as a result of the British naval blockade of Germany during the Great War. More would die whilst the blockade was kept in force after the Armistice of 11 November 1918.

18GW1183 The Allied leaders who made all the major decisions at the Paris Peace Conference, 18 January 1919: David Lloyd George for Britain; Vittorio Emanuele Orlando for Italy; Georges Clemenceau for France; Woodrow Wilson for the United States.

The 'Big Four' of the Versailles Peace Conference: Vittorio Emanuele Orlando, David Lloyd George, Georges Clemenceau and Woodrow Wilson. The French leader was determined to make Germany pay for the devastation caused to his country and the huge loss of life it suffered.

18GW1185 Returning German soldiers withdrawing from the Alsace region cross the Rhine over a pontoon bridge, November 1918. Flags flying, this makes clear that they are not natives of Alsace; band is playing and an officer reviews the march past.

18GW1195 A scene at the Brandenburg Gate, Berlin, as soldiers of the defeated German army receive a heroes' welcome from a crowd of jubilant Berliners. Without a true sense of defeat on the field of battle, for many the scene was set for the another world war.

18GW1187 Occupying French soldiers viewing the covergence of the Rhine and Mosel rivers at Koblenz, from *Festung* Ehrenbreitstein.

18GW1188 British 18th Hussars in Cologne, riding alongside the river docks, 6 December 1918.

18GW1189 American troops cross into Germany as part of the postwar Allied occupation of the Rhineland region.

18GW1196 Field Marshal Sir Douglas Haig arrives at Cologne with General Plumer, who had been appointed commander-in-chief of the British Army of the Rhine in December 1918.

18GW1186 General Currie with his staff leads the Canadians crossing the Rhine..

On 10 November, 1918 German Emperor Wilhelm II crossed the border by train and went into exile in the Netherlands, which had remained neutral. Wilhelm first settled in Amerongen, where on 28 November he issued a belated statement of abdication from both the Prussian and Imperial thrones, thus formally ending the Hohenzollerns' four hundred year rule. Accepting the reality that he had lost both of his crowns for good, he gave up his rights to '*the throne of Prussia and to the German Imperial throne connected therewith*'.

18GW1199 Wilhelm II and his entourage waiting for the royal train at the station in the Dutch border town of Eijsden.

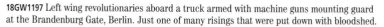

18GW1190 Crowds outside the Reichstag in Berlin 9 November 1918, as the creation of a republic was announced.

18GW1197 Left wing revolutionaries aboard a truck armed with machine guns mounting guard at the Brandenburg Gate, Berlin. Just one of many risings that were put down with bloodshed.

Revolution in Germany was triggered by the Imperial Navy commanders deciding to carryout an all-out operation against the Royal Navy and who issued the naval order of 24 October 1918 for the High Seas Fleet to steam up. Instead of obeying their orders to begin preparations to fight the British, German sailors arose in revolt at Wilhelmshaven on 29 October 1918, followed by the Kiel Mutiny in the first days of November. A spirit of civil unrest spread rapidly through Germany and ultimately led to the proclamation of a republic on 9 November 1918, two days before the armistice.

18GW1202, 18GW1203. German sailors defiant and in open revolt at Kiel. These man are the soldiers' council of the SMS *Prinzregent Luitpold*. The Kiel Mutiny was a major rebellion by sailors of the German High Seas Fleet on 3 November 1918. The revolt triggered the German revolution, which swept aside the monarchy.

18GW1204 Admiral Franz von Hipper; his decision to take his fleet into the North Sea and seek a final battle with the British started a mutiny.

18GW1205 *Schutztruppen* (Protection Troops) for the newly formed *Arbeiter-und Soldatenrat* (Workers' and Soldiers' Council) marching along the Unter den Linden in Berlin. Among them are former sailors and soldiers, along with civilians, all armed and some carrying bandoliers of ammunition.

18GW1206 An old artillery piece mounted on a field gun carriage has been brought into action in the courtyard of the Royal Palace, Berlin, which has been stormed and occupied by representatives of the Soldiers' Council.

18GW1207 Protection Troops of the Workers' Council. A machine gun placed behind a metal sculpture of a turtle, for cover, is manned by a former sailor, a youngster under training and a soldier.

18GW1192 Reels of newsprint and bundles of newspapers used for cover by one group of the warring factions fighting outside a newspaper printing works in Berlin in 1918.

18GW1191 Leftist soldiers during Christmas fights in the Pfeilersaal (columned foyer) of the Berlin City Palace.

18GW1193 The Silesian Railway Station in Berlin was occupied by government troops.

18GW1194 The bodies of revolutionaries who had been summarily executed.

The Russian Imperial Romanov family: Anastasia, Maria, Tatiana, Olga, Tsar Nicholas II, his wife Tsarina Alexandra and Alexis. In the middle of the night, 16-17 July 1918, the family and those who chose to accompany them into imprisonment were shot, bayoneted and clubbed to death in the basemant of a house in Ekaterinburg.

18GW1209 The basement of the house of a local merchant, N N Ipatiev, where the seven members of the imperial Romanov family and their small retinue were killed by the Bolsheviks. The White Army was approaching Ekaterinburg and the sounds of gun fire could be heard in the distance by the royal prisoners and their Bolshevik captors. The arrival of their potential liberators sealed the fate of the Tsar and his family. The wall has been torn apart in the search for bullets to help identify who killed them and how they died.

18GW1211 Yakov Mikhailovich Yurovsky the chief executioner of Emperor Nicholas II of Russia, his family, and four retainers.

18GW1212 Bolshevik leader Vladimir Lenin (wearing a coat around his shoulders) walking across Red Square with his military leaders. Faced with 'White' counter revolutionaries and Allied intervention, the Bolsheviks were forced to expand the Red Army to stay in power.

After Russia made a peace treaty with the Germans in 1918 (Treaty of Brest-Litovsk signed on 3 March 1918) and withdrew from the Allies, it then became torn apart in civil conflict. The Allies intervened on the side of the anti-Soviet White forces to try and restore the Eastern Front. However, lack of domestic support, general war weariness, along with divided aims, compelled the Allies to withdraw in 1920.

18GW1213 Anti-Bolshevik Volunteer Army in South Russia, January 1918.

18GW1214 Vladivostok, Russia. Soldiers and sailors from the countries of the Allied nations lined up in front of the joint headquarters building. The march past is by the Japanese contingent.

18GW1215 General Edmund Ironside. In 1919 he was given command of the Allied intervention force in northern Russia Some 30,000 men, almost half of them British, were stationed at the Arctic ports of Murmansk and Archangel. The campaign lasted from 1918, during the final months of the First World War, to 1920.

18GW1216 A British Lewis gun team in northern Russia in 1918. An American and a Russian soldier are with them.

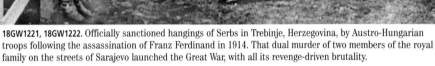

18GW1221, 18GW1222. Officially sanctioned hangings of Serbs in Trebinje, Herzegovina, by Austro-Hungarian troops following the assassination of Franz Ferdinand in 1914. That dual murder of two members of the royal family on the streets of Sarajevo launched the Great War, with all its revenge-driven brutality.

Charles Franz Joseph was the last monarch of the Austro-Hungarian Empire, reigning from 1916 until 1918. He 'renounced participation' in state affairs, but did not abdicate and then spent the remaining years of his life attempting to restore the Hapsburg monarchy until his death in 1922. Austria remained a republic.

18GW1217 Emperor Charles I of Austria-Hungary.

18GW1224 A Communist demonstration on the streets of Vienna being faced by armed Gendarmerie.

18GW1225 Starving Vienna: a queue at the American Food Commission's offices in the winter of 1919-20. Months after the war had ended the continued blockade by the British was having a cruel effect on the people of Austria and Germany.

18GW1220 Seven mutinous soldiers about to be shot. The ethnic Czech units in the Austrian army revolted in May 1918 and their defection was brutally suppressed. It was considered as mutiny by the code of military justice. The Austro-Hungarian Empire was disintegrating.

With Austria-Hungary's declaration of war against Serbia on 28 July 1914, a specially raised corps began conducting mass executions of Serb civilians; in one instance seventy-nine of Trebinje's prominent citizens, among them intellectuals, landowners and members of the clergy, were hung. Killings continued throughout Herzegovina, accompanied by the taking of hostages, looting, and the destruction of property.

18GW1223 Emperor Franz Josef of Austria sought revenge for the assassination of his nephew, Archduke Franz Ferdinand and wife. He died in November 1916, and was succeeded by his grandnephew Charles.

THE DISSOLUTION OF AUSTRIA-HUNGARY. The heavy dotted line bounds the old Austro-Hungarian Monarchy; the light dotted lines show the several provinces. The heavy solid lines bound the new states formed by the Paris Peace Conference as follows: **1**. The Republic of Austria; **2**. The Republic of Hungary; **3**. The Republic of Czechoslovakia; **4**. Austrian territory annexed by Poland; **5**. Hungarian territory annexed by Rumania; **6**. The Serbo-Croat-Slovene State (Yugoslavia). **7**. Austrian territory annexed by Italy.

The Kingdom of Bulgaria fought with the Central Powers from 14 October 1915, when the country declared war on Serbia, until 30 September 1918, when the Armistice of Thessalonica came into effect. In September 1918 the French, British, Italians, Serbs and Greeks broke through on the Macedonian Front during the Vardar Offensive and Tsar Ferdinand was forced to sue for peace. He abdicated in favour of his son Boris III. Bulgaria lost its Aegean coastline to Greece and most of its Macedonian territory to the new state of Yugoslavia. It also had to give Dobruja back to the Romanians.

18GW1217 Ferdinand I, Tsar of Bulgaria, abdicated in 1918.

18GW1224 Bulgarian delegates at the Armistice of Thessalonica: Major General Ivan Lukov, Andrey Lyapchev and Simeon Radev.

The Treaty of Neuilly – signed 27 November 1919 – dictated that Bulgaria should surrender its Mediterranean Sea coastline to Greece; recognise the independence of Yugoslavia; pay reparations of one hundred million pounds; and maintain an army no larger than 20,000 men. As might be imagined, the Bulgarians were strongly aggrieved by the terms of this treaty. On the other hand, were they to consider what their former military partners in the Central Powers had lost, it was lenient in comparison. The treatment meted out to Germany and Austria. would ensure further conflict in years to come. Germany also lost all her colonies in Africa and thus the raw material sources of those lands.

A map of Europe in 1919, showing post-war territorial changes.

18GW1228 Boris III, Tsar of Bulgaria. He acceded to the throne on 3 October 1918.

The scene of the world changed dramatically after 1914. The Great War altered countries, removed dynasties and crafted a new Europe. Three of the continent's most powerful monarchies: the Hohenzollern dynasty in Germany, the Romanovs in Russia and the House of Habsburg-Lorraine in Austria-Hungary, had disappeared. The map of Europe was redrawn; borders were redefined and new countries formed, created from the Russian and Austro-Hungarian empires. Some ethnic and nationalist groups, which had long dreamed of nationhood and self-government, became independent. However, the reconstruction of Europe did not eradicate old prejudices nor presumptions about who should rule and where. The new Europe was an idealistic formation – as was the League of Nations – and they would both fail to withstand the extreme nationalism that was already beginning to ferment soon after the war ended.

The Ottoman Empire entered the war on 29 October 1914, when it attacked targets on Russia's Black Sea coast. Russia responded by declaring war seven days later. Ottoman forces fought the Entente in the Balkans and the Middle Eastern theatre of the Great World. The Turkish defeat in 1918 led to the collapse of the empire. It was stripped of 170,000 square miles of territory. Some was given to Greece and Armenia, while Britain (Palestine and Iraq) and France (Lebanon and Syria) were allocated mandates in the Middle East.

18GW1231 Mehmed VI.

18GW1230 Departure of the former emperor Mehmed VI from Dolmabahçe Palace after the abolition of monarchy, 1922.

Within months of the Great War ending a war erupted between Greece and Turkey. The Greco-Turkish War of 1919–1922 was fought between Greece and the Turkish National Movement during the partitioning of the Ottoman Empire after the First World War. Greece had been promised by the British Prime Minister, David Lloyd George, territory of the deafeated Ottoman Empire. On 15 May 1919, Greek forces landed at Izmir (Smyrna) and moved inland, taking control of part of Anatolia. Their incursion was checked at the Battle of Sakarya in 1921 by the Turks, who counter-attack in August 1922 and the war effectively ended with the recapture of Izmir.

18GW1232 Greek soldiers arriving in the city of Izmir are welcomed by the Greek population, 15 May 1919.

18GW1239 Anastasios Papoulas, commander-in-chief of the Greek Army.

18GW1241 Turkish medics working at a town to rescue wounded after Greek forces abandoned the town on their withdrawal to Izmir, August 1922.

18GW1240 The Great Fire of Izmir (Smyrna) as seen from an Italian ship, 14 September 1922.

18GW1242 Mustafa Kemal's visit to Çay during the Greco-Turkish War 31 March 1922. The Turks were involved in repelling incursions into their territory in other areas and by other nations and were fighting a war of Turkish Independence. From left to right: chief of staff of the Western Front (Greek invasion), Miralay Asim Bey; commander of the Western Front, Mirliva Ismet Pasha; unknown; military attaché for Soviet Russia, Zvonarev; ambassador for Soviet Russia, Aralov; Mustafa Kemal Pasha; ambassador for Azerbaijan, Ibrahim Abilov; commander of First Army, Mirliva Ali Ihsan Pasha.

In 1920, following the Battle of Marash fought between the French and the Turks, the French retreated and Armenian refugees who had recently been repatriated to the city following the Armenian Genocide, estimated to be between 5,000–12,000, were massacred. The deliberate policy of the Moslem Turkish government to annihilate Christians in their empire began in 1915. The Allied Powers of Britain, France and Russia issued a joint statement charging the Turkish government with committing a 'crime against humanity' in reference to that regime's persecution of its Christian minorities. The Greeks also massacred Turks, but on a much smaller scale.

18GW1243 In the Armenian provinces of Turkey in the spring and summer months of 1915 scenes like this were common – the population of entire villages were murdered.

18GW1244 Armenian civilians, escorted by armed Turkish militia, are marched through the town of Kharpert to a prison in the nearby Mezireh district, April 1915.

18GW1245 Talaat Pasha, Turkish Minister of Interior. On 24 April 1915, he ordered the arrest and deportation of Armenian intellectuals in Constantinople, most of them later being murdered. On the 30 May 1915 he instigated the Tehcir Law (Temporary Deportation Law); these events launched the Armenian Genocide. He is considered to be the main perpetrator of the genocide and thus is held responsible for the death of anything between 800,000 and 1,800,000 Armenians.

18GW1246 Djemal Pasha, Minister of the Navy, one-third of the military triumvirate known as the Three Pashas (also called the 'Three Dictators') who ruled the Ottoman Empire during the Great War.

18GW1247 Enver Pasha served in the dual capacity of War Minister and Ottoman Commander-in-Chief during World War One, and was instrumental in bringing Turkey into the war on the side of the Central Powers.

On 3 November 1918 Talaat Pasha and Enver Pasha, the two main perpetrators of the genocide, fled the Ottoman Empire.

18GW1248, 18GW1249. Deportations of Armenians, forced from their homes and force marched until they dropped. The sick, elderly and little children, as always in such cases, were the first to succumb.

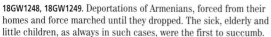

NORTH & CENTRAL
AMERICA
1,075,685 DEAD

EUROPE
2,163,303 DEAD

ASIA
15,757,363 DEAD

AFRICA
1,353,428 DEAD

SOUTH
AMERICA
827,250 DEAD

AUSTRALIA
965,245 DEAD

Global impact of the killer flu

In the spring of 1918 large numbers of soldiers in the trenches in France became ill with sore throats, headaches and loss of appetite. It appeared to be highly contagious. Doctors were unable to identify the illness but eventually they decided it was a new strain of influenza. Soldiers named it 'Spanish Flu' and the name stuck; but there is no evidence that it originated from that country. In Spain they called it 'French Flu', and 'Naples Soldier'. A recent study suggested that the disease was brought to the Western Front by American soldiers from Kansas. In the summer of 1918 symptoms became more severe. Many victims developed bronchial pneumonia or septicemic blood poisoning and a growing number were dying. In one sector of the Western Front over 70,000 American troops were hospitalised and nearly one third of these men died.

By the end of the summer of 1918 the influenza virus had spread to the German Army. The virus created serious problems for the German military leadership as they found it impossible to replace their sick and dying soldiers. The infection spread to the civilian population of Germany and over 400,000 died of the disease in 1918.

In Britain it suddenly appeared in Glasgow in May, 1918. It soon spread to other towns and cities and during the next few months the virus killed 228,000 people throughout Britain. Desperate methods were used to prevent the spread of the disease. Streets were sprayed with chemicals and people started wearing anti-germ masks. However, all treatments devised to cope with this new strain of influenza were completely ineffectual.

In the United States a particularly virulent strain began to sweep through the country. By early December about 450,000 Americans had died of the disease with the total fatalities there coming to some 650,000.

India suffered most: the first cases appeared in Bombay in June 1918, then, in the following month deaths were reported in Karachi and Madras. With large numbers of India's doctors serving with the British Army the country was unable to cope with the epidemic. Between June 1918 and July 1919 upwards of 16,000,000 people in India died of the virus.

Some have estimated that throughout the world over seventy million people may have died of the influenza pandemic.

18GW1251 Recent influenza research into the genes of the Spanish flu virus shows it to have genes adapted from both human and avian (bird) strains. Soldiers plucking turkeys on the Western Front: yet another possible theory as to the origins of the Spanish Influenza Pandemic of 1918.

18GW1252 The Motor Corps of the St Louis chapter of the American Red Cross remove a flu victim during the influenza epidemic, October 1918.

18GW1255 A bus receives a going over with anti-flu liquid. These measures did nothing to stop the spread of the disease.

18GW1256 A street car conductor in Seattle, America, in 1918, refusing to allow a passenger on board who was not wearing a mask.

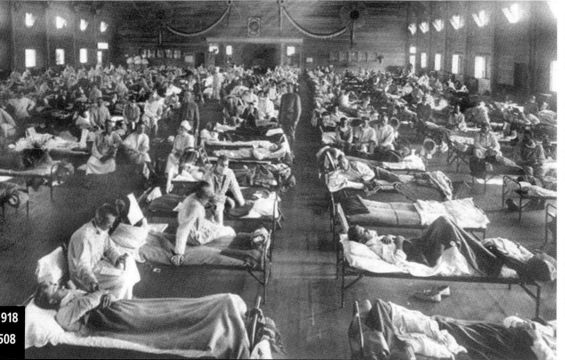

18GW1257 American Expeditionary Force victims of the flu pandemic at US Army Camp Hospital no. 45 in Aix-les-Bains, France, in 1918.

18GW1259 Precautions against the Flu in Tokyo, 1919.

18GW1255 The burial of Spanish flu victims in North River, Labrador, Canada 1918.

EPIDEMIC INFLUENZA (SPANISH)

This Disease is Highly Communicable.
It May Develop Into a Severe Pneumonia.

There is no medicine which will prevent it.
Keep away from public meetings, theatres and other places where crowds are assembled.
Keep the mouth and nose covered while coughing or sneezing.
When a member of the household becomes ill, place him in a room by himself.
The room should be warm, but well ventilated.
The attendant should put on a mask before entering the room of those ill of the disease.

TO MAKE A MASK

Take a piece of ordinary cheesecloth 8 x 16 inches, fold it to make it 8 x 8 inches. Next fold this to make it 8 x 4 inches. Tie cords about 10 inches long at each corner. Apply over mouth and nose as shown in the picture.

ISSUED BY THE PROVINCIAL BOARD OF HEALTH

18GW1261 Two Parisians wearing notices and gauze masks to encourage citizens to take this precaution: *Yes the Boche may be defeated, the flu is not. All wear masks, try it, adopt this.*

18GW1262 With the outbreak of Spanish Influenza in Melbourne in December 1918, Barwon House in Main Street, Mordialloc, Melbourne was converted into an emergency hospital 1919. People were advised not to panic; local authorities were aware of the disease in Europe and its devastating effects upon the population, so strict procedures had been put in place in order to limit its impact. Melbourne escaped relatively lightly compared to other Australian towns and the number of deaths in Europe and America.

Nutrition deteriorated in all european countries during the course of the war. Germany was dependent on food imports, which were stopped by the Allied blockade. At the same time German domestic production of foodstuffs suffered a serious decline. The combination of these two factors led to a massive food crisis. Soup kitchens (*Kriegsküchen*) for children were introduced. Controls were imposed upon nearly all food and fuel. Substitute foods were produced – the unpopular K-Brot, 'war bread' was made from anything from potatoes to straw. The blockade was maintained for eight months after the Armistice in November 1918, into the following year of 1919. Various claims have been made as to the number of deaths in Germany that occured after the war from starvation, from 100,000 to a million. Restrictions on food imports were finally lifted on 12 July 1919, after Germany had signed the Treaty of Versailles.

18GW1263 By 1917 in Germany the nutrition situation had become critical, particularly was it the case in cities: children being fed in a Berlin charity soup kitchen.

The Russian famine began in the early spring of 1921 and lasted through 1922. That deprivation of sustenance killed an estimated two to ten million people (as with other large scale famines, the range of estimates is considerable). The famine came about from the economic upheaval, which had already sprung up during the Great War, and continued through the havoc of the Russian revolution and civil war. Russian communist revolutionary Vladimir Lenin, in charge of the country since 1917, in a chilling disregard for the suffering of his fellow countrymen he instructed food to be seized from the poor, convinced that the peasants were actively acting to undermine the Bolsheviks' interests. By confiscating their food it reduced their ability to harm the revolution.

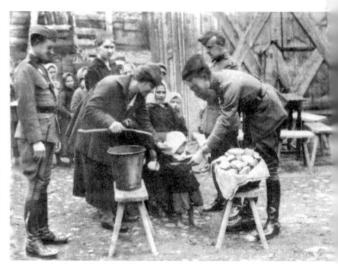

18GW1266 Starving little girl in Buguruslan, Orenburg Oblast, Russia. 1921.

18GW1268 An American relief organization was allowed into the country to work among the famine haunted Russian peasants in 1923.

18GW1267 A couple begging for food with their starving children during the Russian famine in 1922.

18GW1264 As the food shortage in Germany worsened substitute (*ersatz*) foodstuffs were made: coffee made from chicory, herbs, berries, or other mixtures; substitutes for sugar, bread and eggs.

18GW1265 Germans waiting in line for their food ration. The Allied naval blockade meant that food imports were scarce. All foodstuffs grown at home went first to Germany's soldiers, while the rest was rationed to the civilian population.

The British government was reluctant to introduce food rationing, but by late 1917 they concluded there was no choice. The first compulsory rationing began at the start of 1918. It was a success, and the British people had enough to eat for the duration of the war.

18GW1269 A policeman checks the ration books of a youngster outside a butcher's shop in London, March 1918.

18GW1270 National Kitchens were restaurants set up on British Government initiative during the Great War to feed people cheaply, at a time when food supplies were scarce because of the German submarine campaign. By the end of 1918 there were 363 National Kitchens throughout the country.

Around the end of the first century a.d. a prisoner of the Roman Empire on the penal isle of Patmos received a frightening vision of four horsemen riding across the entire inhabited earth, bringing untimely death in various forms to mankind; the vision apparently alluded to a period of world upheaval in the future. *The Four Horsemen of the Apolcalypse* has been a subject capturing the imagination of artists for centuries and many attempts to interpret the meaning by scholars and theologians have been made. The illustration here is based on a painting by Russian artist Viktor Vasnetsov, 1887.

I looked, and there before me was a white horse! Its rider held a bow, and he was given a crown, and he rode out as a conqueror bent on conquest. Revelation 6: 1 to 8 (New International Version of the Bible.)

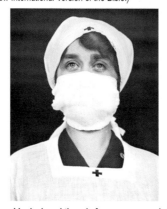

Then another horse came out, a fiery red one. Its rider was given power to take peace from the earth and to make people kill each other. To him was given a large sword.

...there before me was a black horse! Its rider was holding a pair of scales in his hand. Then I heard what sounded like a voice... 'Two pounds of wheat for a day's wages...'

I looked, and there before me was a pale horse! Its rider was named Death, and Hades was following close behind him. They were given power over a fourth of the earth to kill by sword, famine and plague, and by the wild beasts of the earth.

The Great War of 1914-18 was 'great' in many respects: it launched numerous innovative ideas on how human life could be terminated violently and produced the means to employ these on a scale hitherto unimaginable. At the dawn of the twentieth century man had discovered how to achieve powered flight and within a matter of a few short years this was turned into a novel way of killing. Underwater hunter-killer vessels were developed into highly effective ship sinkers. Sea mines; asphyxiating gases; flamethrowers; land crawlers – named tanks – arrived from the drawing boards and laboratories and were employed along with the long established methods of slaughter. Devolment of tactics ensured that new weapons, along with those already in existence, were used to maximum effectiveness: machine guns were skilfully employed to dominate the battlefield; massed artillery pounded enemy positions for days on end and the gunners became more efficient at their craft; even cattle-controlling barbed wire found a new and deadly use where armies faced each other in bitter rivalry. The industrial capability of the belligerents was harnessed and developed as fighting gulped down raw materials. Civilians became embroiled as never before in the history of warfare in the all-consuming aggression. The Great War saw on a grand scale starvation used by both sides as a weapon to bring people (mostly fellow 'Christians') to their knees. State religions promoted the great evil as they scrambled to fan patriotic fevor, supplying their representatives to bless the butchery in the various theatres of war. Atrocities were committed at all levels, reaching the depths of depravity in the mass genocide, 'ethnic cleansing' of the Armenians. The four years of madness was 'great' at every level and gave rise to the forlorn catchphrase: *The War to End all Wars*, made in in 1914 by H G Wells, and which became, eventually, a hollow attempt to give some justification for the human sacrifices suffered.

The pictures above, selected to typify the effect of the symbolic horsemen on mankind, are representative of the hundreds of images that could have been used to show the effects of the Great War: the German machine gun team wearing gas respirators – the **Red horse** and rider who took peace away from the whole earth in 1914; children in Russia, 1920, the **Black horse** and rider rationing out food (these children have been eating grass, straw, tree bark and earth worms and can no longer be saved); the **Pale horse** mounted by Death brings pandemic plague – from 1918 to 1919, Spanish Influenza killed forty to seventy million people, a nurse wearing protection against the killer flu; the 'wild beasts' well describe the perpetrators who introduced mass-extinction of entire peoples to the twentieth century – the severed heads of captives illustrates this horror. And observing mankind in the twenty-first century, we must conclude that the symbolic four horsemen are still out there.

18GW1273 German delegates in Versailles: Professor Walther Schücking; Reichspostminister Johannes Giesberts; Justice Minister Otto Landsberg; Foreign Minister Ulrich Graf von Brockdorff-Rantzau; Prussian State President Robert Leinert, and financial advisor Carl Melchior. Their humiliation and that of the German nation had been decided upon by the victorious Allies.

18GW1275 A crowd surges around Versailles Palace after the signing of the 'Peace treaty' 28 June 1919.

The Treaty of Versailles was negotiated among the Allied powers with little input from the Germany delegation – it was told what it must accept.

The Rhineland demilitarised.

The Saar, with its rich coalfields, given to France for 15 years.

Alsace-Lorraine returned to France.

Germany forbidden to unite with Austria.

Rich farmlands in eastern Germany given to Poland.

Danzig made a free city under League of Nations control.

Germany's colonies given to France and Britain as 'mandates'.

The German army restricted to 100,000 men.

The German navy restricted to six battleships and no submarines.

Germany not allowed to have an air force.

Germany made responsible for causing all the war damage.

Germany to pay reparations – eventually set at 132 billion gold marks.

Terms of the treaty can be classified into three groups:

territorial – provisions that took territory away from Germany
military – restrictions limiting Germany's armed forces;
financial and economic impositions.

18GW1276 Former owners of property in the German colonies protesting on the streets of Berlin about the terms of the Treaty that dispossessed them. *We Germans abroad protest against the violent peace and the theft of our private property.*

The League of Nations. American President Wilson used his influence to attach the Charter of the League to the Treaty of Versailles. He was convinced that an effective League would put to rights any injustice in the peace terms. He and the other members of the 'Big Three', Georges Clemenceau of France and David Lloyd George of the United Kingdom, drafted the covenant for the League as part of the Treaty of Versailles. It proved incapable of preventing aggression by the Axis powers in the 1930s. It lasted just twenty-six years before disappearing at the outbreak of the Second World War. Over two and a half thousand years ago it was recorded: *The course of Man is not in his control, nor is it in man's power as he goes his way to guide his steps.* Jeremiah 10:23 The Jerusalem Bible

!8GW1277 Headquarters of The League of Nations in Geneva, Switzerland, created after the Great War to provide a forum for resolving international disputes. First proposed by President Woodrow Wilson as part of his Fourteen Points plan for peace in Europe, the United States never became a member. The League proved to be ineffective in preventing military aggression.

It is humiliating to remain with our hands folded while others write history. It matters little who wins. To make a people great it is necessary to send them to battle even if you have to kick them in the pants. That is what I shall do.
Benito Mussolini

I have given orders to my Death Units to exterminate without mercy or pity men, women and children belonging to the Polish-speaking race. It is only in this manner that we can acquire the vital territory which we need. After all, who today remembers the extermination of the Armenians?
Adolf Hitler,
22 August 1939.

All this I saw as thoughtfully I pondered what goes on within this world whenever men have power over their fellows, power to injure them.
Ecclesiates 8:10 James Moffatt Bible

To choose one's victims, to prepare one's plan minutely, to slake an implacable vengeance, and then to go to bed ... There is nothing sweeter in the world.
Joseph Stalin 1940.

Our Empire stands at the Threshold of glory or oblivion. Once His Majesty reaches a decision to commence hostilities we will all strive to repay our obligation to him... resolved that the nation united will go on to victory... an all out effort to achieve our war aims.
General Hideki Tojo,
Imperial Conference
1 December 1941.

Index